KU-510-416

WITHDRAWN

N 0007630 9

C87/1

PUBLICATIONS OF
THE NORTHERN IRELAND COUNCIL
FOR EDUCATIONAL RESEARCH
32

MATHEMATICS AND THE MICRO

NEWMAN COLLEGE
BARTLEY GREEN
BIRMINGHAM, 32.

CLASS	375.51
ACCESSION	85625
AUTHOR	DAR

Copyright © *1985*

The Northern Ireland Council

for

Educational Research

MATHEMATICS
AND THE MICRO

A report on the availability and use of microcomputers in
Northern Ireland's post-primary schools and their
application to the teaching of mathematics

by

JOHN D'ARCY

ACKNOWLEDGEMENTS

I would like to express my gratitude to the principals and teachers who took part in this study, especially to those who participated in interviews. Their courtesy and co-operation ensured that this stage of the project was not only informative and interesting but also enjoyable.

The project's Steering Committee, whose members included representatives from the Secondary Mathematics Panel of the Queen's University Teachers' Centre, was supportive and helpful throughout the project's progress. The Committee's Chairman, Mr. S. I. Davidson, merits special mention for his guidance and skilful chairmanship.

Dr. J. Gardner, Department of Education, Queen's University, Mr. B. Evans, N.I. Council for Educational Development and the computer development officers from the Education and Library Boards were generous with their time and advice during the planning stages of the project.

I am grateful to the Department of Psychology, Queen's University, and in particular to Mr. D. J. Hale, for the use of its technology to produce graphics for this report and to the staff of the Queen's University Computer Centre for their help in the preparation of the data for analysis.

Finally, I would like to thank my colleagues in the NICER Research Unit. Special thanks are due to Dr. J. A. Wilson, Research Director, and Dr. I. F. Wells, Senior Research Officer, for their advice, guidance and enthusiasm at each stage of the project. I am also indebted to Mrs. E. J. Butler, Dr. T. P. Foote, Mrs. A. K. Sloan, Mrs. T. McNally, Miss B. J. McMaster and Mrs. A. E. Smythe for their help with the administration of the project.

NICER Research Unit,   *John D'Arcy*
The Queen's University of Belfast

THE STEERING COMMITTEE

CHAIRMAN

Mr S. I. Davidson   Killard House School, Newtownards

SECRETARY

Mrs E. J. Butler   Administrative Officer, Northern Ireland Council for Educational Research

MEMBERS

Mr R. Gribben   Belfast Education and Library Board

Mr P. McCrossan   Royal Belfast Academical Institution, Belfast

Mr W. McCullough   Larkfield Secondary School, Belfast

Mr D. McKeown   Ballycastle High School, Ballycastle

Mr R. Sinnamon   Stranmillis College of Education, Belfast

EX-OFFICIIS

Mr J. M. D'Arcy   Research Fellow, Northern Ireland Council for Educational Research

Dr I. F. Wells   Senior Research Officer, Northern Ireland Council for Educational Research

CONTENTS

Page

FOREWORD . . . . (ix)

Chapter 1: **INTRODUCING THE STUDY**

1.1 The arrival of microcomputers in secondary schools   1

1.2 The need for research on the use of computers in schools 2

1.3 Computers and mathematics teaching . . . 3

1.4 Background to this study 5

1.5 The questionnaire survey 6

1.6 The school visits 8

Chapter 2: **THE AVAILABILITY AND USE OF MICRO-COMPUTERS IN POST-PRIMARY SCHOOLS IN NORTHERN IRELAND**

2.1 Provision of microcomputers in post-primary schools   12

2.2 Types of computers found in schools . . . 14

2.3 Peripheral computer equipment reported by schools   15

2.4 When the microcomputers were obtained . . 16

2.5 The location of microcomputers in schools . . 17

2.6 Variation in provision between schools in different geographical areas 18

2.7 Microcomputer provision within grammar and secondary schools 19

2.8 Providers of microcomputers 21

2.9 School size and microcomputer provision . . 22

2.10 School policies on the use of computer assisted learning (CAL) across the curriculum . . 23

2.11 Microcomputer use in subjects within post-primary schools 26

CONTENTS *(continued)* Page

Chapter 3: **MICROCOMPUTER USE IN MATHEMATICS DEPARTMENTS**

3.1 An indication of microcomputer use in the teaching of mathematics 28

3.2 Topics in which microcomputers were used . . 32

3.3 Policies within mathematics departments on the use of microcomputers 34

3.4 Factors which encouraged mathematics teachers to use microcomputers in their teaching . . . 37

3.5 Factors which discouraged mathematics teachers from using microcomputers in their teaching . 41

3.6 Microcomputer training received by mathematics teachers 46

3.7 Software used in mathematics departments . . 51

3.8 Microcomputer support and advice available from Area Boards 54

Chapter 4: **CLASSROOM PRACTICE**

4.1 Classroom organisation 58

4.2 Three 'user' schools 61

Chapter 5: **SUMMARY AND DISCUSSION**

5.1 Provision of microcomputers in post-primary schools 67

5.2 Microcomputer use in post-primary schools . . 69

5.3 Computer use within mathematics 70

5.4 Factors which inhibited widespread computer use in mathematics 71

5.5 Encouragement to use computers in mathematics . 75

5.6 Conclusions 76

THE MAIN FINDINGS 81

REFERENCES 84

APPENDIX 1 86

FOREWORD

The establishment of the Microelectronics Education Programme in 1980 greatly accelerated the rate of growth of microcomputers in classroom use in Northern Ireland. Many teachers who, at the outset, felt compelled to embrace the new technology are now beginning to feel that the time is opportune to evaluate the contribution which microcomputers have made to classroom practice.

This project was initiated by NICER at the request of a panel of mathematicians who felt that it was important to examine in detail the use of computers in post-primary mathematics education.

The results of this study highlight areas where action will be required if schools are to derive maximum benefit from the use of modern technology in the classroom and it is hoped that the findings will be of assistance in helping to determine future provision of resources and teachers' initial training and inservice needs.

I would wish to record my thanks to the members of the Steering Committee who worked so enthusiastically to complete this project within the planned one year time scale.

Chairman   Ivan Davidson
Steering Committee

Chapter One:
Introducing the study

1.1 The arrival of microcomputers in secondary schools

Advances in microelectronics during the mid-1970's not only dramatically revolutionised the world of computing but also began to influence society in general. In a very short time powerful computing devices became relatively cheap and widely available. The impact of the availability of such devices was also felt in education. The Council for Educational Technology (CET) in the document "Microelectronics: the implications for education and training" (1978) assessed the educational implications of this revolution and made several recommendations which formed the basis of later government-backed schemes.

In 1980 the Microelectronics Education Programme (MEP) for England, Wales and Northern Ireland was established and funded by the Education Departments of these three countries. Although MEP was funded initially for three years, in April 1983 the Government announced its extension until April 1986. For this five year period the programme had a budget of approximately £23 millions.

The aims of the programme, in addition to "helping schools to prepare children for life in a society in which devices and systems based on microelectronics are commonplace and pervasive", were to encourage the use of microtechnology across the curriculum as well as develop appropriate new areas of study. It aimed to achieve this by extensive inservice teacher training, teaching resources and learning materials development, and operating a network of fourteen regional information centres. These centres received further funding from the local education authorities in whose areas they operated.

In August 1985 it was announced that the MEP would come to an end in March 1986. It was intended that the MEP should be replaced by a Microelectronics Support Unit which would act as a central source of information, assist with the training of teachers and develop curriculum materials. In addition to this, a subsidy was announced by the Department of Trade and Industry to assist purchasers of educational software.

Another government initiative which gained considerable attention, The Department of Trade and Industry's "Micros in Secondary Schools" scheme, was announced in 1981. Its initial aim was to ensure that all secondary schools in England, Northern Ireland and Wales would have access to a microcomputer. This was implemented through a matched funding scheme in which the Department agreed to pay half of the cost of a microcomputer system and the remainder being found by the local Education and Library Board, the Department of Education, the school, parents or combinations of these sources. Given the continued help from these local sources, in providing hardware and the initial impact of the national schemes all post-primary schools have now at least one microcomputer. Indeed, the majority of schools have a number of microcomputers.

1.2 The need for research on the use of computers in schools

The arrival of computers in schools has occurred over such a short period that there has been little time to take stock of these developments. Watt (1983) vividly described the situation in schools,

> "Schools are in the grip of a computer mania. Ordinarily conservative and slow to change, schools are embracing new technology and new educational methods more rapidly than they can learn to use them. During the past few years, the influx of microcomputers in education has grown from a mere trickle to a torrent."

The pressures on schools to acquire and use computers have come from a variety of sources. Many parents wish their children to acquire skills which they feel will be of use in a world where computers are commonplace in everyday life. Many educationalists believe that schools should reap the benefits that technology can bring to learning in all subjects across the curriculum.

The potential benefits of using computers in education are widely reported, perhaps most forcefully by Papert (1980). Although many studies on the effectiveness of computer based learning, as compared with traditional teaching, have been inconclusive, Hativa (1984) reports that several recent research reviews, for instance, Kulik, Kulik and Cohen (1980), Burns and Bozeman (1981) and Kulik, Bangert and Williams (1983), using the statistical technique of meta-analysis to integrate findings from such studies, have shown significant increases in student achievement when using computers. Indeed, computers proved to be especially effective when used to supplement traditional teaching in the discipline of mathematics.

In a discussion document published by the Social Science Research Council (now the Economic and Social Research Council), Sage and Smith (1983) addressed research needs in the use of microcomputers in education. In broad terms two research thrusts were proposed. One dealt with Learning Processes and Information Technology (IT). This was a long-term aim in which research should focus on the styles, strategies and processes of learning with IT. The second research thrust was concerned with Curriculum and the Information Society. Sage and Smith argued that research which will contribute to our understanding of these effects and of the issues surrounding the development of curricula for the era of rapid change into which we are now moving must be given a high priority. They suggested that, in the short term, research should investigate the factors which promote or inhibit the uptake of new technology and its application by schools.

Recently, studies which have looked at the impact of computers in schools have begun to appear. A report by the Welsh Office (1984) described a survey undertaken by members of Her Majesty's Inspectorate (HMI) to assess the impact and the possible implications of new technology in schools. The survey involved visits to 35 secondary schools in Wales and details of provision and practice within those schools are provided in the report. Another survey commissioned by the Department of Education and Science and the MEP (BBC Educational Research Unit, currently in press), looked at provision and computer use in a representative sample of secondary schools in England, Wales and Northern Ireland.

1.3 Computers and mathematics teaching

There has been a long association between computers and mathematics, probably stemming from the earliest use of computers to carry out large numerical computations. In the realm of mathematics education there has also been a strong link between the two, since most of the work with computers in schools, from the early sixties onwards, was undertaken by mathematics teachers, often within the school mathematics curriculum.

The Cockcroft Report (1982) recognised the benefits technology can bring to mathematics education and a complete chapter of that report was devoted to the use of microcomputers and calculators. The committee considered that the availability of low cost calculators and micro-computers had very great implications for the teaching of mathematics.

More recently, a discussion paper by Her Majesty's Inspectorate (HMI), "Mathematics from 5 to 16" (1985), pointed out that microcomputers were a powerful means of doing mathematics very quickly and sometimes in a visually dramatic way. The paper stated that microcomputers can be used in at least three ways which often overlap: (a) as a teaching aid, (b) as a learning resource for pupils and (c) as a tool for pupils to use in doing mathematical tasks. In a section on classroom approaches in mathematics teaching, microcomputers and calculators were described as essential resources.

A substantial number of articles have appeared in educational and computing journals about mathematics and computers. A computerised search of the Education Resources Information Center (ERIC) database, using the keywords Computer Based Instruction and Mathematics Education, revealed no fewer than 300 articles. However, a large number of these dealt with computer use at university level.

Most of the articles discussed the general potential of computers in mathematics teaching. An early paper by Brissenden and Davies (1975) suggested that the introduction of comparatively cheap storage display terminals, which cost approximately £2,500, had brought computer graphics within the range of schools. Despite its optimism about the funds available for such resources in schools in 1975, the paper did indicate some areas of mathematics in which the graphical capabilities of the computer could be exploited to good educational effect. It suggested, for example, projectiles, orbits, graphs, histograms, transformation geometry, symmetry, reflections, rotations and translations.

Several papers have described aspects of classroom practice. For example, Philips (1982) described the use of a single computer in a classroom. He suggested that the computer can augment the presentation of a topic by generating examples, summaries, illustrations or questions and can produce such displays rapidly, flexibly and accurately. Ridgway et al. (1984) reported an interesting experiment involving the use of mathematics software. The researchers observed fifteen mathematics teachers using software to aid their teaching of second and third year pupils. Teachers were provided with a collection of over 90 programs, together with suggestions for lessons, and they attended a weekend inservice training course. In return, they agreed to use the software at least once per week, to comment on each program they used and to allow an observer to watch. The observers noted, among other things, which types of software were most frequently used and which lessons went best. Although the researchers expected teachers' interest to be especially high at the beginning of the term and to fall off as the novelty of the machines diminished, they found no evidence of this. Indeed, for most of the teachers the value of the computer appeared to increase during the term as they became skilful at using it. The researchers noted that some lessons were more successful than others, though, considering the experiment as a whole, the value of the microcomputer as a teaching aid was indisputable. It raised pupils' interest, clarified difficult ideas and put more demands on pupils to think for themselves.

A comprehensive treatment of the use of microcomputers is to be found in Fletcher's 1983 discussion paper, "Microcomputers and Mathematics in Schools". The paper described the use of computers in mathematics in both the primary and secondary sector, types of software in use, pupils' responses to using computers and it outlined many implications of microcomputers for mathematics teaching. In the introduction to the paper, Fletcher wrote:

> "The changes which readily available personal computers make to the practice of mathematics are profound. The implications of current technology are so extensive that it is difficult to present a balanced appraisal without seeming to exaggerate. No doubt further developments are still to come, but whatever changes microcomputers may make to mathematical education in the future we may say, beyond all doubt, that some of the changes which they have made already are so big that we lack any previous standard by which to compare them."

1.4 Background to this study

In March 1984 the Secondary Mathematics Panel of the Queen's University Teachers' Centre asked the Northern Ireland Council for Educational Research (NICER) to investigate the use of microcomputers in secondary mathematics teaching. The Panel, which consists of teachers, members of the mathematics inspectorate and other individuals interested and involved in secondary mathematics education in Northern Ireland, felt that it was important to examine the use of computers in secondary mathematics so that information would be available to guide future provision of resources and teachers' inservice needs.

NICER agreed to undertake this project. Among the aims of the study were the establishment of the extent of microcomputer use in mathematics teaching, the description of the nature of usage, the types of teaching involved and the identification of reasons for the use and, especially, the non-use of computers. The study involved a province-wide survey among school principals, which sought details of provision and use of computers throughout each school, and a further survey among all heads of mathematics departments to obtain detailed information on computer use in mathematics teaching. A time scale of one year, beginning in September 1984, was set for the investigation.

The research was planned in two stages. The first consisted of questionnaire enquiries about microcomputer availability and the extent of computer use within the school and the mathematics department. The second stage consisted of interviews which, in addition to obtaining more detailed evidence than by questionnaire, also sought information on the types of teaching involved. A working group made up of members of the Research Council, NICER staff and representatives of the Secondary Mathematics Panel were involved during all stages of the project's planning and in ongoing reviews of its progress. The experience of the group, reflecting their backgrounds as mathematics teachers, school principals, teacher trainers, administrators and researchers, proved to be invaluable during the design of questionnaires and interview schedules for the project.

1.5 The questionnaire survey

Two questionnaires, one for the principal and one for the head of the mathematics department, were designed to collect information from all post-primary schools in Northern Ireland about their use of microcomputers and, in particular, their use in mathematics teaching. The school principals' questionnaire sought information on the availability of microcomputers within the school and a description of those departments within the school which used computers. Principals were also asked if the school had a policy on the use of computers across the curriculum and, if it had, they were asked to outline the objectives of the policy.

The questionnaire for heads of mathematics concentrated on the use of microcomputers in the mathematics department. In addition to seeking information on whether or not microcomputers were used to help teach mathematics, departmental heads were asked to indicate those factors which encouraged and discouraged mathematics teachers from using microcomputers in their teaching and to describe inservice training which members of their department had received.

In designing the questionnaires, drafts were prepared after discussion with members of the Secondary Mathematics Panel, educational computing officers from the Education and Library Boards, colleagues within NICER and other individuals working in the domain of computer education in Northern Ireland. These drafts were considered by the project's Steering Committee, some modifications were suggested and these were incorporated in both questionnaires.

The revised versions of both questionnaires were piloted in eight schools (three grammar and five secondary) for clarity, layout and ease of completion. The piloting took place in mid-October 1984. The principal and head of mathematics in each of the eight schools were sent a copy of the appropriate questionnaire. After a few days these were collected personally by the researcher, who asked the principals and departmental heads about content and layout.

Questionnaires were next sent to each principal and head of mathematics in the province on 22nd October 1984. Each received a questionnaire, a letter outlining the aims of the project and a FREEPOST envelope for returning the completed questionnaire directly to the researcher. The confidentiality of their evidence was guaranteed. By the closing date, 31st October, 46% of school principals and 21% of heads of mathematics departments had returned questionnaires. A reminder letter and a further copy of the questionnaire were sent to each principal and departmental head who had not replied. By the end of December 231 principals (88.5%) and 159 heads of mathematics (60.9%) had replied[1].

The final response figures for both questionnaires are shown in Table 1.5.1. These are presented for areas covered by the Education and Library Boards and also for schools of different management types. Columns headed by P refer to replies from school principals and HM columns refer to responses from heads of mathematics.

---

[1] An investigation was carried out among a one-in-five sample of departmental heads who had not returned questionnaires. It had been suspected that heads in departments which did not use computers may have been unwilling to reply because they felt that they would have little to contribute to the study. However, it was found that non-responding departments did not differ significantly from responding departments in their use of the microcomputer. Rather, the heads of these departments admitted to being too busy to attend to the questionnaire.

Table 1.5.1: *Percentage responses to the questionnaire enquiries across Board areas and types of school*

	Total		Controlled Secondary		Maintained Secondary		Controlled Grammar		Voluntary Grammar	
	P	HM	P	HM	P	HM	P	HM	P	HM
Belfast % Replies	94	54	87	60	94	29	100	67	100	73
North-Eastern % Replies	88	67	84	50	87	69	100	100	92	83
South-Eastern % Replies	95	75	100	73	83	75	100	100	100	75
Southern % Replies	79	51	78	61	71	43	100	60	85	46
Western % Replies	88	59	83	45	84	68	100	50	100	55
OVERALL % Replies	88	61	87	59	83	56	100	76	95	67

The response rates from school principals across regions ranged from 79% (Southern area) to 95% (South-Eastern area). The data indicated that a larger percentage of grammar school principals replied than did those from secondary schools. In terms of overall response the South-Eastern area was best; controlled secondary, controlled grammar and voluntary grammar schools all provided 100% returns. The lowest response rate of all sectors came from maintained schools in the Southern area—their response rate was 71%.

From Table 1.5.1 it is clear that the response from departmental heads was considerably lower than that of school principals. Response rates ranged from 51% (Southern) to 75% (South-Eastern). As in the case of the principals' questionnaire more returns were received from heads of mathematics in grammar schools than from those in secondary schools. Controlled and voluntary grammar schools realised returns of 76% and 67% respectively, while controlled and maintained secondary schools yielded rates of 59% and 56% respectively.

1.6 The school visits

After the questionnaires had been returned, the second stage of the project involved interviews between the researcher and staff of a small sample of mathematics departments throughout the province.

The interview stage had four broad aims:

to validate the evidence obtained by questionnaire;

to gain a clearer insight into the range of ways teachers use computers in their teaching of mathematics;

to establish reasons why some mathematics teachers use computers while others do not;

to obtain evidence from individual mathematics teachers about their experiences with microcomputers in mathematics teaching.

Twelve mathematics departments, from the 159 which had returned questionnaires, were selected to participate in this phase of the investigation. In selecting departments the main criteria were the degree of microcomputer use within the mathematics department and the level of resources within the school. Other factors included balancing the number of grammar and secondary schools in the sample and ensuring that the sample included mathematics departments from across the province. The methods used in deciding on criteria for these factors are described below.

RESOURCES

Pupil-computer ratios were calculated for each department by dividing the number of pupils by the number of microcomputers in the school. For example, a school with 600 pupils and 10 microcomputers has a pupil-computer ratio of 60. Ratios ranged from 17.5 to 707.0 pupils per computer. A bar chart illustrating the distribution of ratios can be found in the first section of Chapter Two (Figure 2.1.2).

Each school's ratio was sorted into one of two groups, Resource-Group One (in which the school's pupil-computer ratio was less than or equal to 100) and Resource-Group Two (in which the school's ratio was more than 100). Nineteen schools for which these data were unavailable were excluded from the sample. Table 1.6.1 shows the number of departments falling into each group.

Table 1.6.1: *Level of computer resources in those schools in which the head of mathematics replied*

	Resource Group One (PCR <= 100)	Resource Group Two (PCR > 100)	No data available	Total
Number of schools	62	78	19	159
% of schools (N = 159)	39	49	12	100

USAGE

Three levels of usage were defined. Level One included all those departments where questionnaire evidence had indicated that microcomputers were not used to help teach mathematics. Levels Two and Three consisted of those departments which reported some microcomputer use in their teaching of mathematics. The difference between Levels Two and Three was one of extent. Level Two departments were those in which less than one third of mathematics staff used microcomputers more than rarely and in which less than half of the forms taking mathematics used microcomputers. Level Three departments included those departments in which more than one third of the staff used microcomputers in their teaching and where more than half of the forms were exposed to microcomputers in their mathematics instruction. Table 1.6.2 indicates how the mathematics departments were classified under this scheme.

Table 1.6.2: *Descriptions of computer use among mathematics departments replying to questionnaire*

	Level One Use	Level Two Use	Level Three Use	Total
Number of schools	87	39	33	159
% of schools (N = 159)	55	24	21	100

SELECTION

When these criteria (resources and use) were combined the resulting Table 1.6.3 provided a means of selecting schools to take part.

Table 1.6.3: *Classification of mathematics departments based on level of provision and computer use*

Degree of computer use	Resource Group One	Resource Group Two
Level Three	11	18
Level Two	20	17
Level One	31	43

Two schools from each cell were chosen, taking account of grammar and secondary representation and ensuring that schools from each geographical area were included.

DESIGN OF INTERVIEW SCHEDULES

A standard interview schedule was developed so as to ensure that each teacher was asked the same questions. This series of questions began with some brief biographical information, for example length of service, number of classes in each form that the teacher took for mathematics and whether or not the teacher also taught computer studies. Since one of the aims of these interviews was to validate evidence obtained by questionnaire, there was some degree of deliberate overlap in the questions asked. Teachers were asked about training they had received on the use of microcomputers, and the degree of encouragement from their principal, head of department or other colleagues to use microcomputers in their teaching. The interviews also sought to provide a further insight into the ways teachers used microcomputers in their teaching. The schedule achieved this by asking questions about topics in which computers were used, how often computers were used, which classes were involved, where the classes took place and details about class organisation when microcomputers were involved.

ARRANGEMENT AND EXECUTION OF INTERVIEW STAGE OF THE PROJECT

Letters were sent to the principal and head of mathematics in each school. These thanked both parties for their co-operation at the questionnaire stage and asked if staff of the mathematics department would participate in the second phase of the investigation. Dates for visits were arranged by the researcher with the head of mathematics.

The number of mathematics teachers in each department ranged between 3 and 11. In schools in which the mathematics department consisted of fewer than five teachers all mathematics staff were interviewed, whereas in larger schools a 50% sample of mathematics teachers were interviewed. These individuals were selected on the basis of information supplied in the questionnaire about their use or non-use of microcomputers and the departmental heads made arrangements for the interviews. Interviews typically lasted between 10 and 40 minutes with each teacher. The twelve schools were visited between 11th and 29th March 1985.

Chapter Two:
The availability and use of microcomputers in post-primary schools in Northern Ireland

The information reported in this chapter was obtained from the principals' questionnaire, which asked for details about each microcomputer in the school. The chapter describes the findings for all schools and then focuses in greater detail on differences between schools across geographical areas, between grammar and secondary schools and on the relationship between school size and microcomputer availability. The chapter also provides details on computer use within schools and illustrates schools' policies on the use of computer assisted learning (CAL) across the curriculum.

2.1 Provision of microcomputers in post-primary schools

NUMBER OF COMPUTERS IN SCHOOLS

Some 231 (88.5%) school principals described 1,431 microcomputers held in their schools. Each school which replied had at least one microcomputer and the largest number in any school was 22. The average number of microcomputers found in schools of all types was 6.2, with a standard deviation of 3.7. The distribution of schools with different numbers of microcomputers is shown in Figure 2.1.1.

Figure 2.1.1: *The range of microcomputer availability in schools*

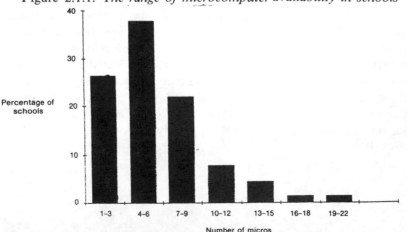

Only six schools (2.6%) had one microcomputer. Of these, one was a grammar school and the remaining five were secondary schools. Over 80% of schools had between two and nine microcomputers each while around 14% of schools had ten or more machines. Although the actual number of computers in a school provides a useful initial indication of availability, the number in isolation from other factors may not be the most useful metric of a school's computing resources.

PUPIL-COMPUTER RATIO

Another way of describing microcomputer provision is to consider the ratio of pupils to each computer in a school. This value is obtained by dividing the number of pupils by the number of microcomputers. This ratio was calculated for each school in the sample. Ratios ranged from 17.5 (pupils per computer) to 707 (pupils per computer). If the extreme case of 707 is omitted from the distribution, the upper limit is reduced to 385 pupils per computer. The distribution of pupil-computer ratios across all schools is shown in Figure 2.1.2. For the purposes of this chart, ratios were grouped into bands of up to and including 50, ratios between 51 and 100 and so on.

Figure 2.1.2: *The distribution of pupil-computer ratios*

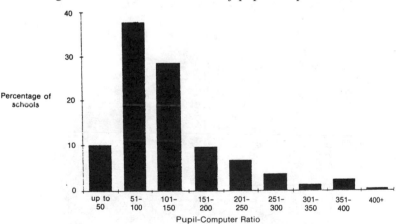

Just under half of the schools (48%) had a pupil-computer ratio of 100 or less, while 38% of schools lay between a value of 101 pupils per computer to 200 pupils per computer. The average ratio was found to be 125.3, although given the wide range of ratios the median value of 104.7 may be a better measure of central tendency. The standard deviation for all schools was 83.

However, it should be borne in mind that the pupil-computer ratio can also give a misleading indication of the school's level of resources. In small schools favourable ratios are produced with relatively few microcomputers, and very large schools with several computers may have poor pupil-computer ratios. Schools with high absolute numbers of machines, even though the pupil-computer ratio is comparatively low, may in practice have greater flexibility as they have more computers available for class use. When considering computer availability as a predictor of the likely pattern of usage, both measures of provision should be taken into consideration.

2.2 Types of microcomputers found in schools

Some 21 different models of microcomputer were described. However, the majority of microcomputers in the schools were accounted for by a small number of models. The percentages of the most commonly found microcomputers are shown in the pie chart in Figure 2.2.1. The bar chart, Figure 2.2.2, represents the percentage of schools with at least one microcomputer of each kind, and this gives an indication of the spread of these machines throughout the schools.

Figure 2.2.1: *The most common microcomputers*

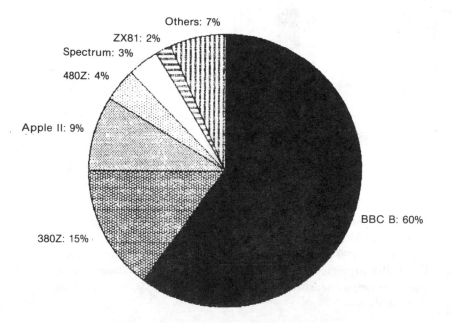

Figure 2.2.2: *The percentage of schools with each sort of microcomputer*

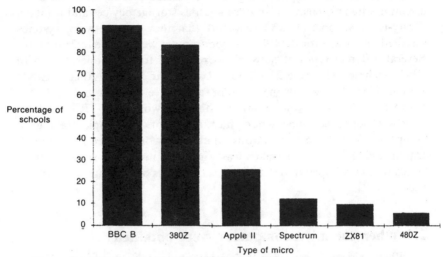

From the pie chart and the bar chart it is clear that the most common microcomputer in post-primary schools was the BBC Model B. It accounted for almost 60% of the 1,431 machines reported and was found in over 90% of schools. The second most frequently found microcomputer was the RML 380Z, which represented 15% of all microcomputers and over 80% of schools had at least one of them. Apple II microcomputers made up 9% of microcomputers reported and approximately one quarter of schools had access to an Apple. Although only microcomputers which each accounted for 2% or more are shown in the pie chart, a complete list of all types of microcomputers reported is to be found in Appendix 1.

2.3 Peripheral computer equipment reported by schools

Information was obtained on the peripheral equipment for micro-computers in these schools. It was found that one-third of microcomputers were cassette based, where programs had to be loaded and saved using cassette recorders. This is a slow and often unreliable way of performing these essential functions. The other two-thirds used the more convenient and reliable disk drives. Just over 40% of the monitors (visual display units) were colour, while the other 58% were monochrome. Only seven schools (3%) did not have a printer and 82% of schools had one or two. The average number of printers was found to be 1.7. Just over one-fifth of schools had either a 'turtle' or a 'buggy' which was used in control technology or with varieties of the programming language Logo.

A' number of schools had a network system, which is a means of connecting several computers together so that they can share the same essential, often expensive, resources such as storage devices and printers. Thirty-three schools (14.3%) reported that they had network systems installed. Networks for the BBC microcomputer were found in 23 schools. Several different types of network were found to be in operation with BBC machines. Of these 23 schools, twelve had a GSL/Ancom E-Net system, eight had an Econet system and three schools had a U-Net network installed. Nine schools had networks of RML 480Z microcomputers and one school had a network of Apple IIe micro-computers. The number of stations on each network ranged from four to fifteen and the average number was eight. A further 23 schools (10%) stated that they hoped to obtain network systems by the end of the school year.

2.4 When the microcomputers were obtained

When principals described their microcomputers, they were asked to state the calendar year when each microcomputer arrived in the school. Dates were provided for 1,386 (97%) of the 1,431 microcomputers described. Figure 2.4.1 illustrates the accumulation of computers year by year.

Figure 2.4.1: *The accumulation of microcomputers in schools*

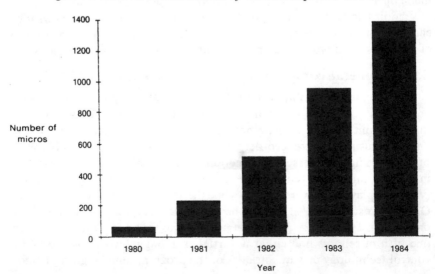

As indicated in Figure 2.4.1, large numbers of computers began to arrive in secondary schools from 1981 onwards, largely as a result of the "Micros in Schools" scheme. This trend has continued as a result of funding from Education and Library Boards, the Department of Education, the schools' own resources and from parental contributions. The net effect has been that, in 1984, the average number of machines in Northern Ireland post-primary schools was 6.2.

2.5 The location of microcomputers in schools

In describing each computer the principal was asked to state where it was located. Details were provided on 1,404 (98%) of the 1,431 microcomputers reported. With schools having an average of six computers each, management decisions had to be made about the locations of these resources. Three main strategies were identified. One strategy was to place all the microcomputers in a single location which can be used by anyone. Another plan was to have one or more microcomputers located permanently in those departments which used computers. A third strategy allowed computers to be moved between locations as demand arose. The 'mobile' computer was a popular option for many schools. Indeed, 35% of the microcomputers listed by principals were described as mobile, whereas the remaining 65% were permanently located in a room in the school. Table 2.5.1 indicates the most frequently mentioned locations for microcomputers.

Table 2.5.1: *Summary of the most common locations for micro-computers in post-primary schools*

Location	Number of schools	% of schools	Total number of micros	% of micros
Computer Room .	168	73	1011	72
Mathematics . .	52	22	135	10
Science . .	32	14	48	3
Physics . .	19	8	27	2
Technology .	10	4	12	1
Other Locations .	99	43	171	12

By far the most common location for the microcomputers was the school's computer room. Indeed, 72% of all microcomputers were housed in computer rooms. In some schools, machines held in the computer room could be brought to other locations as the need arose. The description 'computer room' has a wide connotation, ranging from a normal classroom where computers are kept to a room specially equipped and wired for microcomputers. Some indication of this range can be gauged by considering principals' replies to a further question, "Does your school have a specially fitted computer room?" While 73% of principals reported housing some microcomputers in 'computer rooms', only 46% of principals stated that these were specially fitted. These data would suggest that the remaining 27% of schools were using ordinary classrooms as computer rooms.

The second most common location for microcomputers was the mathematics department of the school, although only 10% of all the microcomputers were housed there. Some microcomputers were also found in science and technology departments. Microcomputers were housed in a further fifteen locations although, since each of these locations was reported by less than ten schools and each accounted for less than 1% of microcomputers, they are included under "Other Locations". Departments in this category included C.D.T., Commerce, Geography, Biology, Chemistry and Social Studies.

2.6 Variation in provision between schools in different geographical areas

Information provided by school principals indicated that there were variations in provision between schools in different areas. In Northern Ireland educational management is divided, at local level, into five geographical areas. For the remainder of this report each geographical area is denoted by the name of the Education and Library Board with responsibility for that area. This does not imply that all microcomputers found in schools in each area were supplied by their local Board, since some schools (voluntary grammar schools, for example) have other sources of funding. Details of microcomputer provision across the main geographical areas are provided in Table 2.6.1.

In terms of the numbers of microcomputers per school, schools in the Belfast area had the highest average (7.3). Belfast schools also had the widest range in terms of numbers of computers found in post-primary schools, from 2 to 22 microcomputers per school. Schools in the North-Eastern and South-Eastern regions each had averages between 6 and 7, and the schools in the West of the province had an average of 5.9 micro-computers. Schools in the Southern region had, on average, the smallest number of computers (4.3).

Table 2.6.1: *Distribution of microcomputers across areas in terms of actual numbers of computers and pupil-computer ratio (PCR)*

	Belfast	North Eastern	South Eastern	Southern	Western
Total number . .	345	362	276	195	253
Minimum number .	2	1	1	1	1
Maximum number .	22	17	18	10	12
Average number .	7.3	6.8	6.4	4.3	5.9
Mean PCR . .	107.4	114.8	112.2	170.8	123.0
Median PCR . .	90.4	94.4	103.7	125.0	108.5
Minimum PCR .	30.8	20.7	17.5	29.4	31.0
Maximum PCR .	336.5	340.0	273.0	707.0	385.0

A consideration of the data on pupil-computer ratios within the areas covered by the five Boards revealed a similar pattern. Schools in the Belfast area had the lowest mean and median ratios (107.4 and 90.4 respectively) and schools in the Southern area had the highest mean and median ratios (170.8 and 125.0 respectively). In each area the BBC Model B microcomputer was the most common machine. Schools in each area had similar types of microcomputers, with the exception of schools in the South Eastern region, which tended to have large numbers of Apple microcomputers but comparatively few RML 380Z machines.

2.7 Microcomputer provision within grammar and secondary schools

Provision in terms of number of computers per school varied between grammar and secondary schools. Table 2.7.1 summarises these differences.

Table 2.7.1: *Number of computers found in grammar and secondary schools*

	Grammar schools	Secondary schools
Total number of microcomputers . . .	573	858
Average number of microcomputers . . .	7.5	5.5

Grammar schools, which represented 33% of schools which replied, had 573 (40%) microcomputers. The number of microcomputers in grammar schools ranged from 1 to 22 and the average number was 7.5. Secondary schools (67% of respondents) possessed 858 (60%) micro-computers. The number of computers in each secondary school ranged from 1 to 18, with an average of 5.5. These differences were also found across the five geographical regions and are summarised in Table 2.7.2.

Table 2.7.2: *Provision within grammar and secondary schools by area*

Area Board	GRAMMAR		SECONDARY	
	Number of micros	Average number	Number of micros	Average number
Belfast . . .	176	9.7	169	5.8
North Eastern . .	146	8.6	216	6.0
South Eastern . .	82	7.4	194	6.1
Southern . . .	81	5.1	114	3.9
Western . . .	88	6.8	165	5.3

Table 2.7.3: *Microcomputer provision by school type by area*

Area Board	Controlled grammar	Controlled secondary	Voluntary grammar	Maintained secondary
Belfast				
% Schools	6	26	33	35
Average number of micros .	6.7	6.8	10.4	5.2
North-Eastern				
% Schools	11	42	23	24
Average number of micros .	9.0	6.3	7.7	5.9
South-Eastern				
% Schools	7	44	19	30
Average number of micros .	6.7	6.9	7.7	4.8
Southern				
% Schools	11	32	25	32
Average number of micros .	5.4	3.5	4.9	4.4
Western				
% Schools	9	21	21	49
Average number of micros .	7.0	6.7	6.5	5.0
OVERALL				
% Schools	9	33	24	34
Average number of micros .	7.1	6.1	7.7	5.1

The pattern was similar in each area, with grammar schools having on average more microcomputers than secondary schools. The difference was most marked in the Belfast area, where grammar schools had an average of 9.7 microcomputers compared with 5.8 in secondary schools. Provision between areas is further confounded by differences in school management, since in each area there were controlled grammar and controlled secondary, voluntary grammar and maintained secondary schools. Provision within each school management type in each area is therefore summarised in Table 2.7.3.

As the data have already shown that grammar schools tend to have more machines than secondary schools, Belfast's higher proportion of grammar schools may have contributed to this area's greater resource level as compared with other regions. From Table 2.7.3, it is apparent that the schools with the highest level of resources were voluntary grammar schools in the Belfast area.

2.8 Providers of microcomputers

Beside each listed microcomputer, principals were asked to indicate the source of funding. Details were provided for 1,382 (97%) of the 1,431 microcomputers described. These data are summarised in Table 2.8.1. The purpose of the table is not to provide a detailed breakdown of the financial contributions made by various parties, but rather to illustrate that microcomputers in secondary schools have come from a variety of sources.

Table 2.8.1: *Percentage of microcomputers supplied by various providers*

Provider	Controlled grammar	Controlled secondary	Voluntary grammar	Maintained secondary
Area Board	46	49	—	47
Board and School . . .	21	22	5	24
School	10	18	17	18
Dept. of Education . . .	1	1	37	1
Dept. of Education and School .	—	—	15	—
Dept. of Industry	5	3	8	4
Donation or Prize . . .	4	2	5	2
School and Parents . . .	7	2	3	2
Parents	—	2	4	1
Dept. of Education and Dept. of Industry	—	—	5	—
Area Board and Dept. of Industry	4	1	—	1
Dept. of Industry and School .	1	1	1	—
Area Board, School and Parents .	1	—	—	—

This table gives an indication of the main providers of micro-computers within each type of school. In many cases, there has been joint funding between, for example, the Department of Education and the school. The main difference indicated in the table is the source of provision in the voluntary grammar sector. Most of the microcomputers were provided for these schools by the Department of Education rather than, in the case of the other types of schools, by the local Education and Library Board.

2.9 School size and microcomputer provision

One factor which is important when assessing the number of computers in a school is its size. Figure 2.9.1 shows a graph which illustrates the relationship between school size and average number of microcomputers in a school.

While small schools (less than 200 pupils) had fewer computers, it is interesting to note the similarity of microcomputer provision for schools of between 401–600 pupils and 601–800 pupils. For schools with pupil numbers beyond 800, the average number of computers rose to almost nine microcomputers. The general finding that the largest schools had most microcomputers was found also to be the case within both grammar and secondary sectors, as shown in Figure 2.9.2.

Figure 2.9.1: *Average number of microcomputers by size of school*

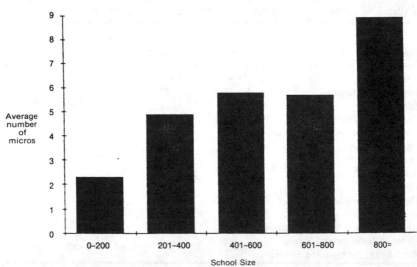

Figure 2.9.2: *Average number of microcomputers by size and type of school*

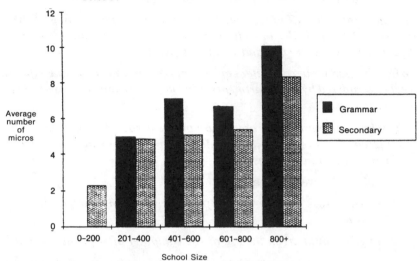

2.10 School policies on the use of computer assisted learning (CAL) across the curriculum

School principals were asked if their school had a policy on the use of computers to assist learning across the curriculum. If a policy existed, principals were requested to briefly outline its objectives. Just over 40% of principals (93) reported that their school had a policy on computer assisted learning. Some 35% of grammar schools had policies, compared with 44% of secondary schools.

When principals outlined the objectives of these policies, it was found that seven broad categories of policy objectives could be identified. In most cases several objectives were mentioned and there were on average two objectives within each policy statement. The remainder of this section describes the main categories of objectives found in schools' policies on the use of CAL. Below each category title is the number of principals who outlined such an objective and the percentage of those principals who described policies with that particular objective. Some examples of policy statements are included under each category to illustrate the types of objectives mentioned by principals.

Encourage CAL across the Curriculum

(85 replies, found in 91% of principals' statements.)

"To encourage all staff to use software packages in the teaching of their subject and to gradually introduce the use of the microcomputer in all departments as experience and resources permit."

"When the fear about computer equipment is overcome, it is hoped that it will be considered by all departments as an aid to learning and used where appropriate."

"The school encourages the use of computers across the curriculum and has placed the stress on using microcomputers outside the narrow confines of computer studies."

"The main objectives will be:

1. *to encourage the use of computers in as many subject areas as possible;*

2. *to give continuity in the use of the computer after primary school;*

3. *to encourage teachers to see the use of computers as a valuable teaching resource."*

"To provide additional learning experience on a departmental basis and to create an awareness of the computer as (a) an investigative tool (e.g., in geography) and (b) a facilitating artefact (e.g., word processing)."

Make resources available

(33 replies, found in 35% of principals' statements.)

"The intention is to equip, as finance becomes available, each department with a microcomputer."

"Financial—fund raising to purchase hardware and software due to the inadequate provision by the Area Board."

"All members of staff are permitted to use the computer in their classroom."

Train teachers to use microcomputers

(30 replies, found in 32% of principals' statements.)

"We are in the process of developing the computer as an audio visual aid. This process takes time and requires basic skills on the part of the teacher. Steps are being taken to provide basic training to a number of staff."

"Teacher training:

    1. awareness and understanding and user competence for all staff;

    2. pool of specialist teachers—four are now qualified;

    3. developing the ability to make informed judgements on software etc."

"Courses are brought to the notice of teachers and in-school training courses have been taken."

To introduce pupils to the new technology

(29 replies, found in 31% of principals' statements.)

"To ensure that all pupils have access to and experience with the use of computers by the time they are 16."

"To introduce pupils to the use of new technology; to familiarise them with it, and to make use of it where it enhances teaching or learning in a purposeful and realistic fashion."

"To improve computer literacy."

Make teachers aware of available software

(11 replies, found in 12% of principals' statements.)

"The main objective is to develop the use of the computer as an aid to learning throughout the curriculum and to draw attention of teachers to the growing pool of available software."

"Staff are kept informed of the availability of software."

Staff responsible for computer development

(2 replies, found in 2% of principals' statements.)

"An appointed member of staff acts as an overall adviser in this area".

"A member of staff is responsible for development in consultation with heads of departments. The aim is to encourage the use of computers across the curriculum."

To produce educational software

(1 reply, found in 1% of principals' statements.)

"To produce good educational software for use in our school and in others."

2.11 Microcomputer use in subjects within post-primary schools

Each principal was asked to list those subjects which made use of the school's microcomputers and to indicate the nature of use within each subject. Details of those subjects which used microcomputers as a teaching aid are shown in Table 2.11.1. Since some subjects, for instance Home Economics, Technology and Craft, Design and Technology, were not taught in every school which replied, the percentage values for these subjects may not truly reflect the amount of computer use in that subject throughout schools.

Table 2.11.1: *Subjects using computers for computer assisted learning*

Subjects	Number of schools reporting computer use in each subject	% of schools (N = 231)
Mathematics	109	47.2
Geography	91	39.4
Science	82	35.5
Physics	47	20.3
Biology	39	16.9
History	32	13.8
Home Economics	31	13.4
English	28	12.1
Chemistry	23	9.9
Commerce	17	7.4
Languages	17	7.4
C.D.T.	16	6.9
Careers	13	5.6
Computer Studies	12	5.2
Art	10	4.3
Technology	7	3.0
Traffic Education	4	1.7
Social Studies	3	1.3
Music	3	1.3
Religion	3	1.3
Humanities	1	0.4

From the data supplied by principals, the subject which made most use of computer assisted learning was mathematics. Almost 40% of geography departments and over a third of science departments used computers in this way. Although the range of subjects employing computers is quite wide (23 subjects) it should be noted that only eight subjects used computer assisted learning in more than 10% of schools.

In addition to using computers as teaching aids with traditional subjects, the machines were also used in other subjects for different reasons. Not surprisingly, the most frequently mentioned subject which used microcomputers was computer studies. As many schools did not have separate computer studies departments, the teaching of computer studies was often the responsibility of other departments. Some 17% of principals reported that computer studies was taught by the mathematics department. In three schools computer studies was taught in the science department. Computer awareness courses were taught in most schools. This is a non-examination subject which aims to introduce pupils to computer technology and its applications in everyday life. This tuition was usually provided by computer studies departments, although in 19% of schools it was provided by the mathematics department. Another use of computers in schools was found in commerce or business studies classes. Although only 7.4% of these departments were reported as using computers for CAL, 28% of principals reported computer use in the commerce department for word processing.

Chapter Three:
Microcomputer use in mathematics departments

3.1 An indication of microcomputer use in the teaching of mathematics

Questionnaires about microcomputer use in mathematics departments were returned by 159 departmental heads. Of the 159 responses, 72 (45.3%) reported that microcomputers were used to help teach mathematics while 87 (54.7%) stated that their departments did not use computers.

Heads of departments which used microcomputers in their teaching of mathematics were asked to give an indication of how often each teacher used microcomputers to help teach mathematics. From the 72 departments which reported some microcomputer use, details were provided on 443 teachers. Table 3.1.1 summarises this information and indicates the percentage of teachers within each category of use. Four categories describing the degree of microcomputer use were indicated in the questionnaire: 'not at all', 'rarely', 'occasionally' and 'frequently'. Percentages are also provided to give an indication of the number of teachers who used microcomputers in all mathematics departments. This calculation was based on the assumption that teachers in departments which did not report computer use belonged in the category "not at all". All respondents had specified the number of teachers who taught mathematics in the department.

The data suggest that even when microcomputers were used, only one quarter of teachers used them more than rarely. While it could be argued that the categories differentiating degree of use are not precise measures of computer use, the data clearly show that more than half the teachers in departments which used computers did not employ them. A consideration of the overall percentages of mathematics teachers indicated that over 80% of teachers did not use microcomputers to help teach mathematics. Replies from heads of mathematics indicated some differences in computer use in different geographical areas. These are shown in Table 3.1.2.

Table 3.1.1: *Degree of computer use among mathematics teachers*

Degree of use	% of teachers in departments which used micros (N = 443)	% of teachers in all departments which replied (N = 1,088)[1]
Not at all	52.4	80.6
Rarely	22.8	9.3
Occasionally	20.3	8.3
Frequently	4.5	1.8

[1] These figures are based on replies from 61% of heads of mathematics in all post-primary schools. The heads gave the number of teachers in each school who taught more than five periods of mathematics per week. Further information obtained from the Department of Education (N.I.) Statistics Branch revealed that over 1,600 teachers teach some mathematics in post-primary schools.

Table 3.1.2: *The number of schools within each area using micro-computers in their teaching of mathematics*

	Belfast	North-Eastern	South-Eastern	Southern	Western
Number of departments using computers in mathematics .	11	19	14	11	17
% of departments using computers in mathematics . .	41	47	41	38	59

The area with the highest proportion of mathematics departments using microcomputers was the Western Board area. Schools in the North-East were the next largest users, followed by the Belfast, South-Eastern and Southern areas.

EVIDENCE FROM INTERVIEWS WITH MATHEMATICS TEACHERS

During the second stage of this project 46 teachers in twelve schools were interviewed about their use or non-use of microcomputers in mathematics teaching. Twenty (43.5%) teachers reported that they used computers to help teach mathematics with some of their classes. The remaining

26 (56.5%) teachers did not use microcomputers, although some of them had previously used microcomputers in mathematics teaching.

When asked how often microcomputers were used in mathematics, most users replied that they were not used on a very regular basis, but rather when the occasion arose. Indeed, teachers found it difficult to estimate how frequently microcomputers were used. In some instances teachers reported that a class would use the computer for a full week when covering a particular topic and then not use it again for a few months. Other teachers used a single microcomputer with a class to introduce a topic or graphically illustrate something which the pupils had already prepared or calculated manually. A few teachers remarked that they only used microcomputers in mathematics at the end of a term for revision purposes.

CHARACTERISTICS OF MATHEMATICS TEACHERS WHO USED MICROCOMPUTERS

Some data based on individual interviews with 46 mathematics teachers are presented in this section on the characteristics of those mathematics teachers who used microcomputers in their teaching (N = 20). As a comparison similar data are presented for those teachers who did not use computers (N = 26).

(a) *Length of service of teachers*

Each teacher was asked to give his or her length of teaching service. Table 3.1.3 summarises the findings for both groups of teachers.

Table 3.1.3: *Length of service (in years) for users and non-users*

	Used computers in mathematics	Did not use computers in mathematics
Number of teachers	20	26
Minimum length of service	2	1
Maximum length of service	25	38
Average length of service	9.4	14.5
Standard deviation	6.8	9.8

The data indicate that those teachers who did not use microcomputers had on average more service than teachers who used computers. Although this particular analysis was only based on 46 teachers, it does suggest that mathematics teachers with longer service may not use microcomputers to the same extent as teachers with shorter periods of service.

(b) *Sex of teacher*

Table 3.1.4 summarises the data available on usage of micro-computers and the sex of each teacher. Among the 46 teachers interviewed, twenty-four were male and twenty-two were female.

Table 3.1.4: *Sex of teacher and computer use*

	Used computers in mathematics	Did not use computers in mathematics
Percentage of male teachers (N = 24)	42	58
Percentage of female teachers (N = 22)	45	55

Among the interviewed teachers there was no difference in computer use on the basis of the sex of the teacher. Instead, the data suggested that similar proportions of male and female mathematics teachers used computers in their teaching.

(c) *Computer studies and computer awareness teachers*

During the interviews teachers were asked if they taught computer studies or computer awareness. Table 3.1.5 summarises the findings among the 46 teachers interviewed.

Table 3.1.5: *Computer studies and the use of computers in mathematics*

	Used computers in mathematics	Did not use computers in mathematics
Taught Computer Studies or Computers Awareness	18	13
Did not teach Computer Studies or Computer Awareness. . . .	2	13
TOTAL	20	26

It is clear from the table that a higher percentage of users than of non-users among the interviewed teachers also taught either computer studies or computer awareness courses. Indeed, 90% of those who used computers in their teaching of mathematics also taught either computer studies or computer awareness classes as against 50% of non-users.

3.2 Topics in which microcomputers were used

The 20 teachers from the interview group who used computers were asked about those topics in which they used microcomputers. They were also asked which topics they would like to cover using microcomputers. In response to both questions, teachers mentioned a wide range of areas.

Computers were most commonly used in graphical work. This particular use employed the unique graphical capabilities of the microcomputer as a teaching aid. These teachers felt that given a resource as powerful as the computer, its facilities should be fully exploited to make topics not easily covered by 'chalk and talk' more possible in the classroom situation. Not surprisingly, several teachers made use of the computer as a processor of numbers, for example in statistics, general problems etc. A list of general topics with which teachers used or would like to use computers is shown in Table 3.2.1.

Table 3.2.1: *Summary of topics covered and topics teachers would like to cover using microcomputers*

Topic	% of teachers who used micros in these topics (N = 20)	% of teachers who would like to use micros in these topics (N = 20)
Graph Work	45	25
Angles	40	—
Statistics/Probability	35	30
Basic Number Skills	30	—
Co-ordinates/Geometry	30	30
Civic Maths	25	20
Equations	25	—
Shape	20	—
Matrices	20	15
Problems	20	—
Fractions/Decimals	20	—
Sets/Venn Diagrams	10	5
General Revision	10	—
Calculus	10	5
Mechanics	10	15
Estimation	10	—
Bearing	10	—
Standard Form	5	—
Vectors	—	10
Investigative work	—	5

During the interviews teachers who used microcomputers were also asked to specify topics or areas which they would like to cover using microcomputers. The teachers pointed out that covering these topics would ultimately depend on software becoming available, or their being made aware that such software existed. Indeed, six teachers said that they would like to cover other topics but could not speculate on what topics these would be, since appropriate software would have to be available. There was a degree of similarity between what some teachers were actually covering with computers and what other teachers would like to cover in the future, given differences in software availability in each school.

MATHEMATICS CLASSES USING MICROCOMPUTERS

' Each teacher interviewed was asked to give details about the classes he or she took for mathematics in each form, and also which classes, if any, used microcomputers. The 46 teachers taught mathematics to a total of 213 classes. However, only 49 (23%) of these classes were taught mathematics with the aid of microcomputers. Information on the number of classes within each form using microcomputers is given in Table 3.2.2.

Microcomputers were used to a greater extent in the lower school. The form which most frequently used microcomputers in mathematics was the third form. From this form onwards the proportion of classes using computers fell until only 10% of form seven classes used computers. However, the data suggest that this was not a gradual fall. Rather, there is a clear distinction between the amount of computer use in forms one to three and forms five to seven.

Table 3.2.2: *Mathematics classes using microcomputers*

Form	Number of classes which used micros in mathematics	Number of classes which were taught mathematics	% of classes which used micros in mathematics
First	9	30	30
Second . . .	8	26	31
Third	12	32	37
Fourth . . .	10	42	24
Fifth	6	46	13
Lower Sixth . .	2	18	11
Upper Sixth . .	2	19	10

3.3 Policies within mathematics departments on the use of microcomputers

Just under one quarter of departmental heads (38) stated in the questionnaire that their department had a policy on the use of computers in mathematics teaching. A further 12 heads (8%) replied that their departments hoped to formulate policies during the school year, and 109 (68%) departments reported having no policy on the use of CAL in mathematics. If a departmental head stated that his or her department had a policy on the use of computers in mathematics teaching they were asked to briefly outline its objectives. In total, 57 policy objectives were outlined by the 38 heads. These objectives could be classified into nine categories.

The most frequently mentioned objective in statements made by departmental heads was to use microcomputers to help teach mathematics. This objective appeared in over half the statements submitted in the questionnaires. The second most common objective was to encourage staff within the mathematics department to use microcomputers in their teaching. Five departmental heads stated that it was an objective within their department to use computers to make mathematics more interesting for their pupils. Two heads reported that it was the policy within their department not to use computers. One of these wanted to keep microcomputer resources free for other departments to use while another suggested that microcomputers would not meet the needs of pupils in his department. Some examples of the policy objectives within each of the categories are presented, with the number of replies falling into each category and the percentage of policies in which each objective appeared.

To help teach mathematics

(21 replies. Found in 55% of policies)

"To reinforce basic skills through another medium."

"To facilitate the learning of mathematics. To illustrate applications. To provide opportunities for open-ended and individual learning situations."

"To eliminate laborious drawings and demonstrations: for example, relating similar graphs, interpreting them and demonstrating the effects of changes in their functions etc."

"To use the microcomputer if it helps in establishing a concept or giving insight into some mathematics process: for example, graph plotting to see effects of changing functions etc."

"To introduce suitable software which will assist the pupil in the formation of concepts and practice in skills, where this can be more effectively achieved than by traditional methods."

Encourage staff to use microcomputers

(16 replies. Found in 42% of policies)

"All teachers within the mathematics department are encouraged to use programs where available and if the computer room is free. An indication of what is available is given to each teacher."

"Teachers are encouraged to use the computer as an extra resource to help provide practice, build concepts, enhance ideas in as many topics in, mathematics as software is available for."

"To have all members of the department involved and convinced of the usefulness of computers."

"Computer assisted learning is to be encouraged where this is shown to be of benefit when followed up by classroom activities."

Make mathematics more interesting for pupils

(5 replies. Found in 13% of policies)

"To stimulate and/or maintain interest in a topic."

"To help pupil motivation. Mathematics must be seen as a lively area of activity and not as a punishment block."

Use with remedial pupils

(4 replies. Found in 10% of policies)

"To stimulate interest in remedial pupils, using the competitive appeal of many programs. To use a more visual approach with some topics."

Obtain microcomputers for the mathematics department

(3 replies. Found in 8% of policies)

"To lobby for the provision of sufficient resources to make it practicable to use microcomputers."

"To increase the numbers of computers and the amount of software as finance permits."

Use for pupils in individual study

(3 replies. Found in 8% of policies)

"To develop a library of software which can be used by individual pupils during private study."

Make software available for staff

(2 replies. Found in 5% of policies)

"To build up a library of good mathematics software which can be used by teachers in class."

Not to use microcomputers in mathematics departments

(2 replies. Found in 5% of policies)

"Not to encourage the use of microcomputers in the department so that they are available for other departments."

Not to use with low ability pupils

(1 reply. Found in 3% of policies)

"Children attending high schools, of whom approximately 5% may attempt 'O' Level, would not be helped by microcomputers."

TEACHERS' PERCEPTIONS OF ENCOURAGEMENT TO USE MICROCOMPUTERS WITHIN THEIR DEPARTMENT

As one of the main aims stated in the policies outlined by heads of mathematics departments was to encourage mathematics staff to use computers in their teaching, teachers were asked during the interviews if they were encouraged to use computers. The twelve departmental heads were not asked this question. The responses of the teachers interviewed are summarised in Table 3.3.1.

Table 3.3.1: *The types of encouragement mentioned by teachers (N = 34)*

Type of encouragement	Percentage of interviewees
Left to self	41
Made aware of available software	32
Made aware of computer availability	21
Still formulating departmental policy	9
Given demonstration	6
Head of department keen for staff to use micros	3

The most frequent type of encouragement mentioned by teachers was of a passive nature. For example, they typically said "It's up to yourself really. The computers are there if you want them". Almost one-third of teachers interviewed stated that they were made aware of available software for mathematics within the school, and they were also given details of what software was available from commercial publishers and Education and Library Boards' software libraries. Just over one-fifth of teachers stated that they were made aware of hardware availability and how to obtain it when needed.

3.4 Factors which encouraged mathematics teachers to use microcomputers in their teaching

Departmental heads were invited to outline up to four factors which they felt encouraged mathematics teachers to use microcomputers in their teaching. Only 36 heads failed to list factors, therefore all percentages presented in this section are based on the replies of 123 respondents. A total of 373 factors were given which were then classified into 15 categories.

Over half of the departmental heads suggested that the availability of good software would encourage mathematics teachers to use computers in their teaching. Although several heads did not fully explain what they meant by good software, some suggested that software should, for example, be educationally sound and that it should match closely what is to be taught according to the syllabus. A number of departmental heads stated that software should be user-friendly, that is it should be easy for the teacher to use in the classroom, with good documentation and clear instructions for use.

The second most frequently mentioned factor was pupil motivation. Half of the respondents felt that the interest shown by pupils when using computers should be fully exploited to make mathematics a more interesting subject for them. The unique characteristics of micro-computers were mentioned by 45% of heads of mathematics departments. Such features as the microcomputer's speed and accuracy of calculation and graphical ability were cited. A similar number of heads stated that better availability of microcomputers would encourage teachers to use computers.

The types of encouragements mentioned by departmental heads and the number and percentage of respondents who mentioned each factor are outlined in the remainder of this section. Examples of statements are also included to illustrate the kinds of encouragements for using micro-computers, as reported by departmental heads.

Good software

(66 replies, 54% of respondents)

"Software packages with good graphics."

"Availability of good software."

"Good software at different ability levels."

"Having suitable software relevant to topics taught in mathematics class."

"Sound educational methods incorporated in software packages."

"User friendly software which is easy to operate."

Pupil motivation

(62 replies, 50% of respondents)

"Computers are stimulating for the class to use."

"Good use of sound and colour can be highly motivating for pupils."

"Gives motivation to the pupils."

"It is a way of making maths more enjoyable. It can make 'boring' topics seem less 'boring'—good source of revision."

"High visual appeal stimulates and motivates pupils."

"Motivation: children of today are generally interested in computers, computer games and gadgetry and so computers provide a vehicle for learning with interest."

Characteristics of microcomputers

(56 replies, 45% of respondents)

"Curve sketching quickly done, projectiles, three-dimensional geometry."

"By saving time on tedious calculations, pupils can concentrate on the concept."

"Speed and elegance of drawing graphs compared with board work."

"Large realistic calculations performed rapidly and long term simulations demonstrated in a short space of time."

"To show three-dimensional diagrams which are otherwise difficult to produce."

Availability of microcomputers

(55 replies, 45% of respondents)

"Ready access to suitable facilities in school."

"Availability of hardware, i.e., number of microcomputers available within the school for this type of use. Ideally a fully equipped room specially for computing and timetabled for mathematics periods. The use of high quality software which is much better at developing a child's understanding of a topic than conventional methods."

"Access to machines."

"Smaller classes."

"Ease of access to microcomputers."

Useful teaching aid

(47 replies, 38% of respondents)

"Can be a useful educational tool."

"Allows for easier investigation."

"Encouraging pupils to get the computer to do something sometimes helps pupils understand the mathematics involved."

"Would give variety in presenting basics again and again to slow learners."

"Allows time to concentrate on small groups of pupils, for instance weaker pupils."

Knowledge of how to use computers

(33 replies, 27% of respondents)

"Personal confidence with the computer."

"Familiarity with how to use micros."

"The ability to set up the computer and load software."

Pupils can use outside normal class time

(11 replies, 9% of respondents)

"Possibility for individual pupils or groups to work on their own."

"Given sufficient microcomputers pupils can be grouped in 'teach yourself' situations, thus enabling the teacher to move around the room and administer individual tuition."

Up-to-date teaching method

(9 replies, 7% of respondents)

"Teachers can update their own expertise."

"Need to keep abreast of current developments."

Teacher interest in microcomputers

(8 replies, 6% of respondents)

"Teacher interest in computers."

"Teacher's enthusiasm."

Teacher awareness of uses

(7 replies, 6% of respondents)

"Some knowledge of how to use computers in the maths lessons."

Evidence of proven worth

(7 replies, 6% of respondents)

"Teachers need to know if computers will actually do any good."

Opportunities for less able pupils

(6 replies, 5% of respondents)

"The opportunity to give less able pupils the opportunity to participate more."

More preparation time

(3 replies, 2% of respondents)

"Time to prepare the equipment for the particular lessons and gain experience."

Other teachers using computers

(2 replies, 2% of respondents)

"Contact with other teachers using microcomputers for mathematics."

Money available to buy software

(1 reply, 1% of respondents)

"Finance to buy our own software."

Interestingly, there were no differences in opinion between heads whose departments used microcomputers and those whose departments did not. Both groups of respondents described the same factors, with much the same emphasis. Factors such as pupil motivation, availability of good software and the characteristics of microcomputers were most frequently mentioned. Although non-users mentioned the availability of hardware more than users did, departments which used microcomputers did not have, on average, more computers in school than those departments which did not. The main difference lay in the rate of responding to this particular question: two-thirds of the heads whose department did not use computers as against with a 90% response rate from heads whose departments did use them.

3.5 Factors which discouraged mathematics teachers from using microcomputers in their teaching

Departmental heads were asked to list those factors which they felt discouraged mathematics teachers from using microcomputers in their teaching. Nine respondents did not complete this section of the questionnaire, thus percentages are calculated on the basis of the 150 departmental heads who replied. 530 discouragements were supplied by heads of mathematics, compared with 373 encouraging factors. The discouraging factors were classified into 12 categories.

The most frequently mentioned discouraging factor was a shortage of microcomputers. Over 80% of departmental heads mentioned this as a factor. A related discouragement, listed by 51% of heads, was the problem of getting access to computing resources because they tended to be used a lot by other departments, usually computer studies. Some 61% of heads reported that they felt many teachers did not use computers because they were unfamiliar with them and needed proper training. Some departmental heads suggested that this unfamiliarity had resulted in teachers being afraid of microcomputers. Over half of the heads cited a lack of good software as a major discouraging factor. A lack of time to prepare lessons using microcomputers and to try out software was reported by more than a quarter of departmental heads.

The sorts of discouragements mentioned by departmental heads are outlined, with the number and percentage of heads who listed each one. Some examples of statements made by respondents are included to give a better impression of those factors which, in the view of departmental heads, discouraged mathematics teachers from using microcomputers.

Lack of microcomputers/large classes

(122 replies, 81% of respondents)

"Unavailability—this I feel is the factor which decides whether or not microcomputers are used in the teaching of mathematics. The majority of my department would welcome the addition of a microcomputer into their classroom."

"The problem of large classes—very difficult for all pupils to see small screens."

"Mathematics classes are usually large—not enough machines to cope."

"A shortage of monitors, thus making it difficult for large classes to see what is being demonstrated."

"Quite honestly, I think improvements must come in the number of computers available in the school. Nothing less than a 2:1 ratio is acceptable—very quickly followed by a 1:1 ratio."

"The small number of computers relative to class size."

Lack of knowledge about computers

(92 replies, 61% of respondents)

"Lack of confidence in using microcomputers as a result of no training."

"Lack of understanding or fear of machines themselves."

"Lack of inservice courses on the teaching of mathematics through the computer."

"Some teachers fear the thought of using a microcomputer if they have no training."

"Unfamiliarity of some teachers with computing and hence a 'fear of the unknown' is harboured by these individuals."

"Lack of guidance on how to exploit the good facilities of the microcomputer and not just to use it as a textbook for revision or consolidation."

Lack of good software

(79 replies, 53% of respondents)

"Absence of suitable software."

"Poor software—plenty of it about."

"Lack of suitable software—most programs are geared for individual use."

"Lack of decent educationally sound software which does not curtail the teacher but enables him or her to provide a beneficial experience for the pupils."

"Suitability of material to individual class needs."

"I feel that the mathematics software available is not outstanding enough to make the effort to use it."

Access to microcomputers/organisational problems

(76 replies, 51% of respondents)

"There are only specific times when the hardware is available."

"Hassle of arranging access to machines."

"Problem of location—classes would need to move to a computer room which is already very heavily used by computer studies classes."

"Difficulty in organising classroom. Using computers means dividing class, those at keyboard and others."

"Computers in school are usually being used by students of computer studies."

"Organisational difficulties, e.g., computer not available when needed."

Lack of preparation time

(42 replies, 28% of respondents)

"Lack of time—teachers under pressure find it difficult to find time to (a) review programs, (b) familiarise themselves with the operation of software, (c) organise themselves, (d) plan lessons using this tool and (e) plan follow-up work."

"Lack of time to evaluate suitable software."

"The extra time required to prepare a lesson involving computer software compared with the more traditional presentation."

"Inadequate training in the use of packages which leads to extra preparation time which in many schools is not available to staff."

Teacher complacency

(27 replies, 18% of respondents)

"Reluctance to change teaching methods."

"Unwillingness of certain teachers—difficult to move from old teaching ways etc."

"A reluctance to forsake the traditional methods when the novelty has no examination relevance."

No contact with other teachers

(22 replies, 15% of respondents)

"Rarely get opportunities to meet other teachers and discuss what use they make of computers."

"No other teachers in locality using micros in this way—we don't know where to start."

Lack of knowledge about software

(21 replies, 14% of respondents)

"Unaware of what software is available."

"Lack of knowledge of types of software available and where to obtain it."

High cost of hardware and software

(18 replies, 12% of respondents)

"Lack of money to buy software and to duplicate handouts to accompany such work."

"Lack of finance to purchase adequate software and hardware."

Examination pressures

(16 replies, 11% of respondents)

"Syllabuses for O-Level, Additional and A-Level mathematics leaves little time for fun or playing."

"Large class groups and pressure to follow a syllabus."

Lack of proven worth

(11 replies, 7% of respondents)

"Unconvinced of their worth."

"With time at a premium staff need convincing that CAL in mathematics would result in greater numeracy and better understanding of the mathematical processes."

Pupils not interested in microcomputers

(4 replies, 3% of respondents)

"Only 50% or fewer pupils show interest."

As with those factors which encouraged computer use, there were no differences in the factors listed as discouragements by heads of departments which used or did not use computers. Problems caused by large classes, small numbers of computers and a lack of knowledge of how to use them were most frequently mentioned. However, there were some differences in the stress put on certain discouragements by heads of departments in different parts of the province. These differences are listed in Table 3.5.1, with the number and percentage of schools in each Area Board which suggested that reason. The number of mathematics departments from each area which replied to the questionnaire is given in brackets.

Table 3.5.1: *Differences between Area Boards*

Area Board	Lack of micros % of depts	Lack of knowledge about micros % of depts	Access problems % of depts	Lack of good software % of depts
Belfast (N = 27) .	59	70	44	44
North-Eastern (N = 40)	47	52	47	32
South-Eastern (N = 34)	56	56	32	59
Southern (N = 29)	62	65	28	52
Western (N = 29)	65	48	38	62

Lack of hardware was of greater concern to mathematics departments in the Southern and Western areas than to departments in the North-East. Fewer departmental heads from the Western area mentioned teachers' lack of knowledge of computers as a discouraging factor. Access problems were mentioned most frequently by departments in the Belfast and North-Eastern areas. (Data presented in Chapter Two indicated that schools within these two areas had higher average numbers of computers than schools in the other areas.) Finally, the data suggest that departments in Belfast and the North-East were less troubled about a lack of good software than mathematics departments in other areas.

EVIDENCE FROM INDIVIDUALS ON FACTORS WHICH DISCOURAGED MICROCOMPUTER USE

The 26 teachers who did not use microcomputers in their teaching of mathematics were asked why they did not use them. A range of reasons were given, and some teachers gave several factors which discouraged them from using computers. The principal reasons are listed in Table 3.5.2.

Table 3.5.2: *Reasons why some teachers did not use computers to help teach mathematics (N = 26)*

Reasons	Number of teachers	% of teachers
Available software inappropriate	7	27
Unfamiliar with microcomputers	5	19
Location of micros in school	5	19
Had used but no longer does so	4	15
Did not feel microcomputers useful	3	11
Not enough microcomputers	3	11
Lack of time to use computers	3	11
No better than traditional methods	3	11
Software too expensive	2	8
Micros used extensively by other subjects . . .	1	4

There was considerable similarity between the discouraging factors suggested by departmental heads and the reasons for non-use given by individual teachers. The software problem was mentioned frequently by both groups, as was the problem of many teachers being unfamiliar with microcomputers and how they might be used in mathematics classes. Five teachers mentioned that the location of microcomputers within the school was problematical. For example, some teachers who taught in mobile classrooms said that the schools' computers were housed in the main building, to which they would have to bring the whole class but which was at least five minutes' walk away. They felt that, in terms of lost class time and the need to book the computer room in advance, computer use for them was ruled out. Other teachers reported that in their school the computer room, in addition to being a central resource, was also the classroom for the computer studies teacher. Although the computer studies teacher was very willing to exchange rooms when another member of staff wished to use the computers, they said that they did not like to interrupt and 'evict' this teacher.

3.6 Microcomputer training received by mathematics teachers

In the questionnaire, heads of mathematics departments were asked to list inservice training courses with microcomputers which members of their department had attended. They were asked to supply details on the number of teachers attending each course, its location and an indication of its duration. Some 117 (73.6%) departmental heads described 237 courses and these were classified into ten types. Table 3.6.1 shows the number and percentage of departments reporting participation on each type of course.

Table 3.6.1: *Departmental participation on microcomputer training courses (N = 117)*

Type of Course	Number of depts	% of depts
Introduction to computers	68	58
Diploma or Certificate in Computer Education . .	43	37
Computers in mathematics	37	32
Programming	28	24
Computer studies	25	21
Computers in education	17	14
Using hardware	9	8
Using software	7	6
Primary degree/teacher training	2	2
Control technology	1	1

The most frequently reported course by departmental heads was a general "Introduction to Computers" course and almost 60% of departments which had mentioned training courses listed this type of course. Less than one-third of departments reported taking part in courses dealing explicitly with the use of microcomputers in mathematics, although a further seven departments described courses which looked at mathematics software. Programming courses and those specifically dealing with computer studies were mentioned by 24% and 21% of departments respectively. Only two departments mentioned that staff had received training as part of their degree or teacher training course.

LOCATION OF MICROCOMPUTER TRAINING COURSES

As indicated in Table 3.6.2, only 17% of departments mentioned courses which had taken place within their school. The majority of courses had taken place outside school, particularly in local teachers' centres, but also in further education colleges and universities.

Table 3.6.2: *Locations of training courses*

Location	Number of depts which reported courses there (N = 117)	% of depts which reported courses there
Local teachers' centre	83	71
Further education colleges	63	54
Universities	61	52
School	20	17
Teacher training colleges	10	8

COURSE DURATION

Just over half (51%) of the training courses reported lasted one week or less. Indeed, 45% of these courses were held on one day or part of a day. Slightly more than one quarter of courses were held over a term, when they consisted of a few hours each week for a number of weeks. The Diploma course was offered on a full-time and part-time basis over a period of one or two years respectively. One year full-time courses represented 7% of all the training courses reported, while part-time versions accounted for 14% of courses.

TEACHERS TAKING PART IN TRAINING

When listing each course attended by members of their staff, departmental heads also indicated how many members of their department had attended each course. Table 3.6.3 summarises this information and the number of mathematics teachers attending each type of course is given. It is possible that individual teachers attended more than one course, as indeed was quite likely in departments where one teacher was considered to be the 'computer expert'. These teachers attended courses and on return to the school hoped to share the expertise with other teachers in the department.

Perhaps the most striking figure from this table is that only 52 mathematics teachers have been on courses which covered the use of microcomputers in the mathematics classroom. Given that 1,088 teachers taught mathematics in the 159 departments which replied to the questionnaire, this suggests that only 5% of mathematics teachers received computer training for their own subject area. There were also differences across the five main regions in the province in terms of the numbers of teachers who attended inservice courses on the use of the computer in mathematics.

Table 3.6.3: *Numbers of teachers attending training courses*

	Number of mathematics teachers who have attended courses	% of mathematics teachers who have attended courses (N = 373)	% of all mathematics teachers in survey (N = 1088)
Introduction to computers.	149	40	14
Programming	56	15	5
Computers in maths .	52	14	5
Diploma or Certificate in Computer Education	42	11	4
Computer studies	33	9	3
Computers in education	18	5	2
Using software .	10	3	1
Using hardware .	5	1	0.4
Control technology	4	1	0.4
Primary degree or teacher training	4	1	0.4

Table 3.6.4 shows for each Board area the number and the percentage of mathematics teachers who attended computer courses dealing with the use of computers in mathematics teaching.

Table 3.6.4: *Mathematics teachers in each area who received training on computers in mathematics*

Area Board	Number of mathematics teachers who attended such courses	Number of mathematics teachers who have attended any computer course	% of attending maths teachers who received training on the use of computers in mathematics
Belfast	6	109	5.5
North-Eastern	9	58	15.5
South-Eastern	10	72	13.9
Southern	11	74	14.9
Western	16	60	26.7

The data suggest that training on the use of computers in mathematics, as compared with other inservice courses, was most common in the Western region and least frequent in the Belfast area.

EVIDENCE FROM THE INTERVIEWS

Evidence was also obtained about inservice computer training for mathematics teachers during individual interviews. Of the 46 teachers interviewed, 35 (76%) teachers had received microcomputer training while 11 (24%) teachers had not received any training. It was clear that there was a strong relationship between some microcomputer training and the use of microcomputers in mathematics. Two-thirds of those teachers who did not use computers had received some training, while 95% of the teachers who used computers in mathematics had received training.

POSSIBLE IMPROVEMENTS TO TRAINING

Departmental heads were asked to suggest any improvements or modifications to the types of training on offer to mathematics departments. Seventy-nine departmental heads offered 140 suggestions, which were classified into 14 categories. Table 3.6.5 indicates the findings.

Table 3.6.5: *Suggestions for improved courses*

Suggestion	Number of suggestions	% of respondents (N = 79)
Practical courses	32	40
Software exhibitions	24	30
More courses	23	29
Courses on mathematics	12	15
School-based courses	9	11
Local courses	7	9
Introductory courses	7	9
Follow-up courses	6	8
Related to education	4	5
Better publicity	3	4
Outside school day	2	2
Courses on hardware	1	1
Financial support	1	1
Meet computer development officer	1	1

The most frequent suggestion from departmental heads was for practical courses that show how to use the computer in the mathematics classroom. A call for software exhibitions was also noted from heads, who saw a need for a regular forum in which teachers could see what software was available, either from Education and Library Boards or from publishers, try it out and then be able to decide whether or not it might be of use to them in the mathematics classroom. There was a clear demand for more courses and also follow-up courses as it was felt that "one-off" training sessions were not sufficient to properly inform teachers about computers and what they could do, and to encourage teachers to think about using computers in their teaching. Some departmental heads, from the more rural areas of the province, asked for courses to be held locally rather than in Belfast, as distance was an important discouraging factor for many teachers, especially after a full day's teaching or during their free time at weekends.

3.7 Software used in mathematics departments

In the questionnaire, departmental heads were asked to list items of software used to help teach mathematics in their department. Of the 72 departments which reported some microcomputer use, 62 provided information on software. Each departmental head who replied listed an average of 3.9 software packages; these 244 descriptions referred to 127 individual packages. Many of the packages listed were not found to be in common use, for example 101 packages received only one reference, and 11 received two references. The three most common items were each referenced 25, 18 and 10 times respectively. While the majority were commercially available items, just under one quarter (23%) were written by individual mathematics teachers in particular schools. These programs were typically cited only once.

Most of the software described tended to be used by younger pupils. 'Junior' classes, 11-14 year olds, and 'Middle' classes, 14-16 year olds, used over 80% of the software packages mentioned by departmental heads. From Table 3.7.1 it is evident that relatively few packages were used by older pupils, in particular those pupils taking 'A' Level examinations. Such details were provided for 214 of the 244 packages listed.

Table 3.7.1: *Age ranges of pupils using mathematics software*

	Junior (11–14 year-olds)	Middle (14–16 year-olds)	Senior (16–18 year-olds)	All pupils (11–18 year-olds)
Number of programs (N = 214)	85	90	27	12
% of programs . . .	40	42	13	5

Some 13% of the software described was used with 16–18 year-olds, including pupils studying for O-Level mathematics as well as A-Level pupils. Indeed, although not specified in the table, only 5% of the software described was used with A-Level pupils. These findings agree with other information obtained by questionnaire and interview, which indicated that microcomputer use in mathematics was concentrated among younger pupils.

Many departmental heads also provided information on the ability levels of pupils using the software they described. In total some 230 ratings of ability were collected; 78% of these were supplied by departmental heads in secondary schools. The ratings can be divided into two types—some heads described the pupils' abilities with terms such as "remedial or below average", "average" and "above average"—143 descriptions of this sort were found. This type of description was used more often by secondary departmental heads, 75% of whose replies came in this form.

A second type of description, of which 79 were collected, used examinations which particular classes would be taking as an indication of their ability. These categories were "CSE classes", "O-Level classes", "O- and A-Level classes" and "A-Level classes". This type of rating was preferred by grammar school respondents, and 72% of replies from departmental heads in grammar schools used this type of ability description.

Both measures provide a similar pattern of results, which is summarised in Tables 3.7.2 and 3.7.3. The tables also indicate differences between grammar and secondary mathematics departments in terms of the reported ability levels of pupils using mathematics software.

Table 3.7.2: *Use of software with different ability groups*

Ability levels	OVERALL		Grammar		Secondary	
	Programs	% (N = 149)	Programs	% (N = 14)	Programs	% (N = 135)
Remedial or below average	46	31	0	0	46	34
Average	92	62	11	79	81	60
Above average	11	7	3	21	8	6

Particularly noticeable from Table 3.7.2 is that although 34% of the programs described in such terms by secondary mathematics heads were used with remedial and below average pupils, none of the programs listed by grammar departmental heads was used with pupils in this ability range. This finding may reflect the differences in academic ability of pupils within each type of school.

Table 3.7.3: *Use of software with different examination classes*

| | OVERALL | | Grammar | | Secondary | |
Examination level	Programs	% (N = 81)	Programs	% (N = 36)	Programs	% (N = 45)
CSE . . .	27	33	0	0	27	60
O-Level . .	35	43	18	50	17	38
O- and A-Level .	14	17	13	36	1	2
A-Level . .	5	6	5	14	0	0

The data from both types of description provide a similar pattern of results. Within each type of school, grammar and secondary, the software listed by heads was not used as much with senior and higher ability pupils as with pupils who were younger and of average or below average ability.

Departmental heads were asked to supply a usefulness rating for each piece of software they listed, as follows: 1—"not useful", 2—"of limited use", 3—"useful" and 4—"very useful". Respondents supplied ratings for 213 of the 244 items they described. Just under half of the software ratings were described as being "of limited use", and 3% were rated as "not useful". One quarter were described as "useful" and 23% of ratings fell into the "very useful" category.

Although some pieces of software were used by several departments, many were only mentioned by one department. The more frequently mentioned software packages were:

Microcomputers in the Mathematics Classroom (Longman) — This package contains 14 teaching units designed to enable teachers to explore the possibilities and potential uses of the microcomputer in mathematics teaching. Some departmental heads described individual programs from this collection and these were also classified under the same heading. This package was listed by 25 departmental heads. It was rated by 21 respondents and ratings ranged from 1 to 4, with an average of 2.9. This collection of programs was mainly used with pupils aged between 14 and 16 years, although some departmental heads reported some use with both Junior (11–14) and Senior (16–18) classes.

DART (AUCBE) — This is a package implements Logo-type graphics on a BBC microcomputer. Eight departmental heads listed this package and their ratings ranged from 3 to 4 with an average usefulness rating of 3.6. The main users of this package were pupils aged between 14–16 years.

Microprimer (Tecmedia) — This is a collection of programs. Four packs of Microprimer are available and most of the software listed from respondents came from Pack 2. Twenty departmental heads listed it and each provided a rating. The ratings for Microprimer ranged from 2 to 4 and the average usefulness rating was 2.7. This suite of programs was only used in Junior classes, with 11–14 year olds.

Approximation, Estimation and Standard Form (Heinemann) — This package aims to develop mathematical skills of approximating numbers, estimation, and conversion of floating point notation to standard form and vice versa. Eight departmental heads listed this package and seven of them gave it a rating. Its ratings ranged from 3 to 4 and its average usefulness rating was 3.3. Most departmental heads reported that this package was used with 14–16 year old pupils.

3.8 Microcomputer support and advice available from Area Boards

Departmental heads were asked to list the support and advisory services provided by the local Education and Library Board and to suggest any improvements that they felt could be made to these services.

Some 167 responses were outlined from 112 heads (70.4%). The responses fell into two categories, those which briefly described some of the services provided by the Board and those which commented upon those services. Comments were made by 72 (64.3%) departmental heads and descriptions of services were given by 95 (84.8%) of the 112 who replied in this section. Table 3.8.1 summarises the descriptions of services available from the Boards.

Some 34% of departmental heads mentioned that their Board employed a development officer to help schools with their micro-computers. The second most frequent description covered the support provided by Boards in regard to software. Schools mentioned software libraries, catalogues provided by Boards detailing software available for schools, and also that the Board provided some free software. These are all included under the heading of 'help with software'. Schools in three Boards, mainly the North-Eastern but also the Southern and Western, mentioned that their Area Board had computer units. Some 14% of departmental heads mentioned that their Area Board provided inservice microcomputer training for teachers.

Table 3.8.1: *Descriptions of computer advisory services provided by Education and Library Boards. (N = 95)*

Type of Service	Number of respondents	% of respondents
Computer advisory personnel	32	34
Help with software	29	30
Provide courses	13	14
Advice on hardware problems	11	12
Computer unit	9	9
Buy hardware	1	1

The range of comments about these services are listed in Table 3.8.2.

Table 3.8.2: *Comments on the computer advisory services provided by the Education and Library Boards (N = 72)*

Comments	Number of respondents	% of respondents
Board provides good facilities	32	44
Not aware of Board's facilities	17	24
Facilities are limited	14	19
Not sure what is available for voluntary schools	5	7
Nothing specifically for mathematics teachers .	2	3
Do not use services	1	1
Services are not needed	1	1

Although 44% of schools which replied to this section described the services offered by their Boards as good, almost one-quarter of departmental heads stated that they were unaware of any services provided by their Board. Almost one-fifth of departmental heads reported that they felt the services provided by their Board were limited.

IMPROVEMENTS TO BOARDS' COMPUTER SERVICES SUGGESTED BY DEPARTMENTAL HEADS

Departmental heads were invited to suggest improvements or modifications to the services provided by their Board. Thirty-two suggestions were made by 30 (19%) departmental heads and these were classified under nine headings. Table 3.8.3 lists these suggestions and indicates the number of departmental heads suggesting each type of improvement.

Table 3.8.3: *Improvements suggested by departmental heads*

Suggestion	Number of respondents	% of respondents (N = 30)
Better contact with schools	15	50
Better location for Board's computer services .	5	17
Regular catalogue of available software . .	5	17
Practical support	2	7
Other Boards provide a better service . .	1	3
Help for voluntary schools	1	3
Better repair facilities	1	3
Special introductory courses	1	3
Examine use of computers in mathematics .	1	3

By far the most frequent suggestion from mathematics departments was for better contact between Board and schools with regard to the services available from Boards. Five departmental heads felt that Board's locations for microcomputer resources should be more central. Some departmental heads suggested that the Boards operate a mobile software library service which would travel around rural schools. Five schools asked for regular, up-dated catalogues of software to be sent out to schools.

USE OF BOARD-PROVIDED SOFTWARE LIBRARIES BY MATHEMATICS DEPARTMENTS

In addition to describing general services offered by their Boards, heads of mathematics departments were requested specifically to comment upon any software library facilities provided by the Area Board. This section of the questionnaire was completed by 117 heads of mathematics (73.6%) and the findings are summarised in Table 3.8.4. As with their responses to the question on general facilities, respondents' answers fell into two camps: those describing the service and those commenting on it. Descriptions of services were provided by 81 respondents, while 109 departmental heads offered comments on the software libraries.

Table 3.8.4: *Descriptions of software library services*

Description	Number of respondents	% of respondents (N = 81)
Lending service	46	57
Send out a catalogue of available software .	21	26
Inspection service is available	7	9
No software for the more able students . .	2	2
Some free software is available	2	2
Software is evaluated	2	2
Available software not useful	1	1

The most frequent description of the software library service highlighted the facility for teachers to borrow software and try it out, and almost 60% of heads described this. The second most common description outlined a catalogue of software items available from the library. Table 3.8.5 summarises comments about Board software libraries.

Table 3.8.5: *Comments on the software libraries*

Comment	Number of respondents	% of respondents (N = 109)
Do not use library	39	36
Facilities are good	32	29
Do not know about software library . .	23	21
Choice is limited	7	6
Library is too remote	4	4
Library being established	2	2
Not sure what is available voluntary schools .	2	2

More than one third of departmental heads reported that their department did not make use of the software library provided by the Board. Almost 30% of heads stated that they felt the library facilities provided by their Board were good. However, one fifth of departmental heads reported that they did not know about the software library. Some reasons for non-use were mentioned as comments, for example "choice of software is limited" and "library is not in a convenient location".

Chapter Four:
Classroom practice

4.1 Classroom organisation

In each of the twelve mathematics departments visited, those teachers who used microcomputers were asked how their classroom organisation changed when they introduced microcomputers. Three main types of change emerged, the first two resulting from computer use in the normal mathematics classroom, where a computer was permanently available or, more usually, when one was brought to the room by the teacher. The other type of organisation was apparent in those schools in which the computing resources were centralised in a computer room, and classes were brought from the mathematics classroom to this location. Details of the types of organisation described by teachers and the problems associated with each are summarised in the following sections.

COMPUTERS IN USE WITHIN THE MATHEMATICS CLASSROOM

Two general types of computer use were reported when microcomputers were brought to the mathematics classroom or when they were located there. Both required different organisational strategies on the part of teachers.

a. *Whole class demonstration*

Several teachers stated that they used the computer to introduce new topics or demonstrate concepts. In instances like this the compuer was being used as an 'electronic blackboard', with pupils grouped around the monitor so that they could all see the demonstration. A major difficulty was arranging the children so that each pupil could see the computer display as easily as possible. Typically, teachers abandoned the more usual arrangement of rows of desks in favour of a semi-circular formation of pupils around the monitor. Some teachers said that this could lead to disruption in the class though, when faced with the prospect of not seeing the computer demonstration, pupils tended to behave themselves.

The most common problem mentioned by teachers using this method was the legibility of the display. Most schools had a twelve inch or fourteen inch monitor and this was not suitable for use by a class of between 25 and 30 pupils. Some teachers mentioned that they would borrow a large television if one was available. However, the problem was then that screen resolution and clarity were not as good as with the monitor, even though the images were larger.

As an example of this kind of usage, consider a lesson dealing with plotting graphs from equations. The teacher may present the class with an equation and then suggest changing the values of the variables in the equation. Class discussion will ensue about the likely changes this will make to the shape of the graph. When the teacher is satisfied that enough discussion has taken place, the computer can plot the graph and the actual changes can be seen on the screen. This result can then lead to further discussion and manipulation of the values of the variables. Teachers typically used this type of presentation to introduce topics which demanded complex or frequent illustrations. The benefits were that diagrams could be produced quickly, accurately and dynamically.

b. *Pupil use*

The second type of computer use within the mathematics classroom involved individual pupils or pairs of pupils using a software package in a corner of the room while the remaining pupils did other work. Teachers stated that with this type of computer use they would let one or two pupils use the computer at a time. These pupils would use the computer for between 5 or 10 minutes with that particular piece of software. When they had finished, another pair of pupils would commence work with the microcomputer. The remaining members of the class would do other work with the teacher. Given this type of use, it would take at least two 35 minute periods to give each member of a 24 pupil class an opportunity to use the software even for this limited time.

These types of lesson typically involved the use of drill and practice programs. This type of use allows, ideally, individual or small groups of pupils to practice elementary arithmetical and algebraic skills of various kinds. Teachers said that they found this approach useful for reinforcing basic mathematical skills and for revision. Many of the programs involved some element of game playing which kept the attention and interest of pupils while they were carrying out what would, more usually, be a somewhat boring chore. Some teachers tried investigative work using this method of organisation. Using software such as DART, pupils can easily program the computer to draw patterns and pictures, and by changing the values of angles and distances produce different results on the screen. Teachers remarked that this type of pupil experimentation was useful since by changing the sizes of angles and values of variables which constructed the patterns on the screen, pupils obtained practical experience of mathematical concepts and relationships which would be more difficult to represent on paper.

In the schools visited, teachers reported that they had to bring the microcomputer to their classroom to use it. In one school the microcomputers were held in a security store at night as a precaution against burglary. This meant that if a teacher wanted to use the computer during the first period it had to be taken from the store, brought to the classroom, set up for use, and the appropriate software loaded so that the mathematics lesson could begin. This took time and often class time was lost, even during the day when the computer might be in a nearby classroom. Teachers stated that typically ten minutes of class time could be lost during the transportation of systems.

The other major problem was the management of both types of teaching during one lesson. In addition to minimising distraction between both sets of pupils, teachers not only had to monitor the progress of pupils at the computer, but also keep the rest of the class engaged in other work. Most teachers tried to use the topics covered in the computer program as work which pupils could prepare before using the computer, carry out at the computer and then assess after they had been on the computer. This approach was particularly prevalent with DART. The main benefit reported by teachers for this sort of computer use was that pupils got some opportunity to use the computer although, given that only one machine was usually available, their amount of 'hands on' experience during lessons was quite low.

c. *Mathematics in the computer room*

The most common location for computer use within the 'visit sample' of schools was a dedicated computer room. This was, in theory, a central resource to which different subjects or departments in the school could have access. Computer rooms ranged from standard classrooms in which a number of microcomputers were housed to specially fitted and wired rooms capable of holding a number of networked machines.

Six of the twelve visited departments which used computers had computer rooms. The average number of microcomputers held in these was 5.6, and the numbers in individual computer rooms ranged from 3 to 9. Two of the schools had microcomputers networked, while the others had individual machines. In many computer rooms the machines held there were not of the same type, so that there were occasions when all the resources of the computer room could not be used—for example if the particular piece of software which the teacher wanted was only available for one microcomputer.

The type of use in computer rooms was predominantly pupil centred. In other words, pupils interacted with the machines rather than simply watching a demonstration. The general pattern of organisation described by teachers was to bring the mathematics class to the computer room and divide the pupils across the available machines. Thus, in a school with nine microcomputers and a class of 30 pupils there were three, sometimes four, pupils at each machine. In a computer room with six machines, five pupils used each microcomputer. In one school which had only three machines in its computer room, one teacher used a strategy which involved establishing four groups within a class of 24 pupils forming a circular pattern of use which ultimately allowed each pupil to have some use of the computer. Thus, during each lesson, three groups of pupils were using computers while one group did desk work.

Teachers in this setting typically played a roving role in the computer room, spending some time with the group of pupils at each microcomputer. If the software was drill or revision based, the teacher would check on the pupils' progress. When more open-ended software was employed, for example DART, the teacher might also suggest further experiments or problems for pupils to try.

4.2 Three 'User' Schools

SCHOOL ONE

School One was a controlled secondary school which was attended by some 800 pupils. The school had 13 microcomputers, an RML 380Z obtained in 1981, a BBC Model A and eleven BBC Model B microcomputers in 1982. More recently, in mid-1984, a network system was installed in configuration with ten of the school's BBC Model B machines. Nine of these computers were used as workstations for pupils, and the other acted as a fileserver for the system. The network system and the microcomputers were held in the school's computer room, which could be booked by any department. The room usually had to be reserved one week in advance and it could be booked in half-hour units.

Ten teachers taught some mathematics and a representative sample of five teachers were interviewed about their use of computers in mathematics teaching. All the teachers said that they were encouraged by the head of department to use microcomputers in their teaching. Staff were informed about the availability of hardware and given details about the department's collection of mathematics software. Catalogues of software from publishers and the local Board's software library were made available to mathematics staff.

In addition to the encouragement given by the departmental head, another member of the mathematics staff was particularly interested in using computers to help teach mathematics and was a source of advice and information to other teachers. This teacher regularly visited the software library, which was organised by the Education and Library Board for the area, in order to borrow mathematics software to use or try out in the school.

Two teachers did not use computers at all in their mathematics lessons. One of them, who believed that microcomputers would not make a useful contribution, stressed that it was important for pupils to see the processes involved in calculations and computations rather than having the results presented instantly by the computer. The other teacher had used the computer two years ago to help teach co-ordinates. The programming language BASIC was used to allow pupils to program computers to draw patterns on the screen. This exercise involved pupils planning their diagrams on squared paper, noting the co-ordinates of the points which made up the pictures and then writing BASIC programs which used these co-ordinates to reproduce the diagram on the screen. This teacher's reasons for not using computers at present related to insufficient free time, because of extra administrative duties, to plan lessons and arrange for computing facilities. However, the use of computers in the future was not ruled out.

The teachers who used microcomputers all tended to use the computer room facilities. Usually all nine workstations were used and this resulted in two or three pupils sharing each microcomputer. However, one teacher, in addition to using the full facilities of the computer room, sometimes brought one microcomputer to a normal classroom to demonstrate topics. In this situation pupils would gather round the microcomputer and watch the demonstration, take part in a general discussion and then return to their usual classwork.

All the teachers felt that their facilities were very good although if it were possible it would be better to have a maximum of two pupils per computer. It was felt that although pupils benefited from working with each other at the computer, the benefits were lost if too many pupils had to use the one machine. Staff in this department felt that it was useful having the computers in a central location and found that the booking system worked quite well. Indeed, several teachers saw it as a useful way to plan lessons with classes.

During classes in the computer room, once the software was operational and pupils had been given instructions on what to do, teachers tended to move among groups of pupils. They monitored their progress, answered questions and offered advice.

Most of the problems encountered with computers were of a functional nature, such as getting programs to load and run. Teachers pointed out that these difficulties mainly occurred when they had to use cassette recorders to load programs into the computer. However, with the use of disk drives and more recently a network system, these problems had disappeared. Although teachers felt that the network was very useful, they pointed out that some software would not work on it.

Although mathematics was taught in each of the first five years, leading to CSE examinations in Form Five, microcomputer use was mainly restricted to Forms One, Two, Three and Four. Pupils in Form Five who were taking CSE examinations did not use them, although some non-examination Fifth Form pupils were able to do so.

Teachers reported that in most cases the microcomputers were not used on a regular basis. They were only used when teachers thought they would be of value with certain topics. Indeed, some teachers said that they might use the computer with a particular class twice a week for a month and then not use it again for a few months. Microcomputer use largely depended on the availability of software which corresponded with the topics being covered.

SCHOOL TWO

This was a maintained secondary school which had some 300 pupils enrolled. In 1982 the school obtained an RML 380Z microcomputer and in 1984 acquired a second machine, a BBC Model B. The school did not have a computer room and therefore the microcomputers were brought to classrooms when required. At the end of each day the machines were returned to a security store.

Three members of staff taught mathematics and each of them was interviewed about the use of microcomputers. The head of department encouraged the use of the school's resources and kept staff informed of available software, both within the school and at the software library provided by the Education and Library Board. The head had made frequent trips to the library to borrow software for evaluation and use in the department. The departmental head also learned about mathematics software from mathematics teachers in other schools.

One teacher did not use microcomputers at all in mathematics. This was not as a result of any unwillingness to do so, rather the reason lay with this teacher's lack of knowledge about how to use computers. Indeed, it was felt that the computer could be a very useful tool with the remedial classes he taught. The teacher would have liked to participate in a course on the use of microcomputers, particularly on their use in remedial mathematics. It was further explained that the small number of computers in the school contributed to his non-use of them so far. Neither computer was available at times when the teacher could experiment with it.

The other two mathematics teachers both made use of a micro-computer in their teaching. Although the school had a BBC microcomputer as well as a 380Z, it had only a supply of mathematics software for the 380Z. In addition, since the BBC microcomputer was used much of the time by computer studies classes, these mathematics teachers only used the 380Z machines for mathematics lessons. According to both teachers, there was no need to book the machine as they could arrange details of its use between themselves.

The 380Z microcomputer, since it was not permanently located in either a central resource room or a particular classroom, had to be set up for use by teachers in their own classrooms. Both teachers reported that typically between five and ten minutes of class time could be lost during this operation. However, they also indicated that the extra benefits derived from computer use more than made up for these organisational difficulties.

The most common method of computer use for both teachers was as a demonstration tool. During such lessons pupils were grouped around the microcomputer's screen to watch a display. Teachers usually tried to use the school's normal television set so that pupils would have a larger visual display for the demonstration. However, they sometimes were unable to borrow this item and consequently the class had to make do with the smaller monitor. A second type of use allowed pairs of pupils to have 'hands on' experience of mathematics software with the computer.

Five forms were given lessons in mathematics and the computer was used with each form. However, examination classes in the fifth form did not make much use of the computer, and then it was only used on rare occasions for revision purposes. Both teachers said that the computer was not used on a particularly regular basis with classes. One teacher stated that sometimes it would be used every day for a week, then perhaps it would not be used again for a month when it might simply provide a demonstration during one lesson. The main determining factor, as widely reported by teachers in this school also, was whether there was software available to help cover a topic.

SCHOOL THREE

School Three was a voluntary grammar school attended by approximately 400 pupils. The school's nine microcomputers were an RML 380Z and an Apple II, both obtained in 1981, a Sinclair Spectrum, acquired in 1983, and five BBC Model B microcomputers and an Electron, introduced in 1984.

Eight members of staff taught mathematics and four of them were interviewed. Each teacher mentioned the encouragement given by the head of the mathematics department. In addition to informing staff on the availability of hardware and mathematics software, the departmental head also actively tried to obtain independent hardware resources for the department. The reason for this initiative was to improve access for mathematics teachers. Mathematics classes were held in mobile classrooms at quite a distance from the main school where the computer room was located. Classes also had to walk across uncovered parts of the school to get to the computer room and, in addition to losing class time, the head felt that this was an unsatisfactory arrangement for pupils, especially during bad weather. A further problem arose from the fact that the computer room was used as a normal classroom by the computer studies teacher. Consequently, when a mathematics teacher wanted to use the room the other teacher had to take his class elsewhere. Although the computer studies teacher was very willing to do so and actively encouraged other teachers to use the resources, several mathematics teachers did not think that it was fair to ask this teacher to move out and so they tended not to use the room as often as they might want to.

The computer studies teacher, who also taught mathematics, further encouraged teachers to use microcomputers. In addition to keeping a catalogue of software available in the department, details of new software borrowed from the regional MEP centre were passed on to staff. This teacher hoped to provide in-school training sessions to familiarise staff with the use of the computers in subjects across the curriculum, including mathematics. Another aim was to develop a resources centre which would have a microcomputer available so that teachers could try out software or for practice with the machine in private.

Only one interviewee did not use microcomputers in the classroom. Although this teacher believed that microcomputers could make a valuable contribution to the teaching of mathematics, logistical problems such as those described earlier hindered the use of computers.

The other teachers interviewed made some use of microcomputers in their teaching. One teacher, who also taught computer studies, used the five BBC microcomputers with first and fourth form classes, usually when the lesson spanned a double period. The other microcomputers were not used because of lack of software compatibility between the machines. This teacher tended to use the computer mainly for revision purposes in such a way that one pupil would be assigned to each computer and work there for approximately five minutes.

Some of the other teachers interviewed used the computers in a different manner. Instead of giving pupils one to one experience with the microcomputer in a rotational fashion, they had small groups of pupils at each computer. Some teachers felt that this was a useful way for the pupils to learn and discuss mathematics.

Although mathematics was taught to A-Level standard in the sixth form, computer use was mainly restricted to first, second, third and sometimes fourth form pupils. The main reason for not using computers with pupils in form five and onwards was that they were examination classes with a full syllabus to cover. Another factor mentioned by some teachers was that there was not much software available for A-Level pupils.

Chapter Five:
Summary and Discussion

5.1 Provision of microcomputers in post-primary schools

This study examined the use of microcomputers in mathematics teaching in the post-primary schools of Northern Ireland. As well as establishing the extent of computer use in mathematics departments, the project also sought details of the type of teaching involved, and an indication of factors which encouraged and discouraged teachers from employing computers in their teaching.

Almost 90% of all post-primary school principals in the province supplied information on the microcomputers in their schools. Although some schools reported having obtained microcomputers in 1980 and before, their arrival in most schools can be traced back no further than 1981. The average number of machines has increased steadily over the years to the point when this survey was carried out in October 1984. At that time, the average number of computers in each post-primary school was 6.2.

Although the average number of machines was approximately six, considerable disparity was found between schools. For example, the number of machines in each school ranged between one and twenty two. Variation in provision was observed across several dimensions. For instance, the type of school, grammar or other secondary, was one source of variation. Grammar schools had on average 7.5 microcomputers compared with 6.5 machines in secondary schools. Even within grammar and secondary schools different levels of provision could be identified. While controlled grammar schools had an average of 7.1 micro-computers, grammar schools in the voluntary sector had an average of 7.7 machines. As for secondary schools, there was an average of 6.1 machines per school in the controlled sector and 5.1 microcomputers per school in the maintained sector.

School size was a further factor which influenced the level of resources within schools. In general, the larger the school the more microcomputers it possessed and similar size trends were found within both the grammar and secondary sectors.

The geographical location of schools produced further differences in resource levels. Averages ranged from over seven machines for schools in the Belfast area to four machines per school in the Southern region. Indeed, by considering several of these factors together, the data indicated that schools with the largest numbers of computers were voluntary grammar schools in the Belfast area. Conversely, schools with the lowest average number of computers were controlled secondary schools in the Southern area.

The most commonly found microcomputers in schools across the province were the BBC Model B and the RML 380Z machines. Indeed, over 90% of schools had at least one BBC microcomputer and over 80% had one 380Z or more. This finding is not surprising as both machines were sponsored under the Department of Trade and Industry's "Micros in Schools" initiative which began in 1981. This scheme, through matched funding with either local education authorities or schools themselves, was largely responsible for the introduction of microcomputers into schools. Subsequent provision has come from local Education and Library Boards, the Department of Education, schools, parents and various combinations of these sources.

There was one major difference in the types of microcomputer found in Northern Ireland schools compared with the rest of the United Kingdom. This was in the large number of Apple II computers reported, and indeed this was the third most common machine in Northern Ireland. While they were found in approximately one quarter of schools in Northern Ireland and accounted for 9% of microcomputers in this study, they were not mentioned in any significant quantity in a survey among a representative sample of schools across the United Kingdom (BBC Educational Research Unit, in press). In Northern Ireland, Apples were particularly common in the South-Eastern Education and Library Board area, where they accounted for almost 40% of microcomputers in these schools. Their wide availability in that area can be explained by the Board's decision to initially supply Apples to its schools, although the BBC B microcomputer has now also become widely available in the same schools.

The evidence suggested that many schools have adopted a strategy whereby their computing resources were kept in a central location which could be booked by teachers for use with their classes. Over 70% of all microcomputers were held in computer rooms, and over 70% of school principals reported that some, if not all, of their schools' machines were housed in such places. Over half of the schools which had computer rooms stated that these rooms had been specially fitted for computer use. Computer rooms in the remaining schools were typically ordinary classrooms. In 14% of schools network systems, which allow several machines to share common resources such as memory and output devices, had been fitted in the computer rooms.

5.2 Microcomputer use in post-primary schools

Just over 40% of principals stated that their schools had policies on the use of computers throughout the curriculum. The most common objective was the encouragement of teachers to use computers in their teaching. The importance of providing adequate levels of hardware and software and making them available to teachers was also mentioned. As part of their overall policy, principals further listed the necessity of training teachers how to use the technology. A common goal of many of the policies outlined was to introduce pupils to the new technology in as many ways as possible.

The most common use of computers was in computer studies, a subject which can now be taken to examination level by pupils in most schools. In addition to introducing computers and their applications, these courses also involved some programming. Another type of course frequently given under the umbrella of computer studies was one in computer awareness. These were typically less formal, non-examination courses in which pupils were introduced to the uses of computers in everyday life. These were given, in most cases, by computer studies teachers, although in many schools computer studies was not yet a department in its own right. As over 70% of principals mentioned that their "computer studies department" used computers for both computer studies classes and computer awareness classes, it is likely that some principals included non-formal departments in their replies, i.e. computer studies teachers who were based in other departments. Computer studies and awareness classes were provided in several schools by other departments, and mathematics departments were reported by almost one fifth of principals as providing computer studies lessons.

Although 23 different subject areas were listed as using micro-computers, it is clear that computer use was concentrated in a few subjects, typically computer studies, mathematics, sciences, history, geography and commercial studies. However, it is encouraging to find that a wider range of subjects, such as languages, art, music and religious education, have started to use computers in their teaching. Since it was only in 1984 that schools had on average six machines, it may not be so surprising that only small numbers of schools reported use in non-science subjects. It may be that only as schools' resource levels rise will other departments and subjects have the opportunity to make use of the microcomputer.

5.3 Computer use within mathematics

In terms of using computers to help enhance the learning of 'traditional' subjects on the curriculum, the subject mentioned most often by school principals was mathematics. Microcomputers were reported being used in this way for mathematics in just under half of the post-primary schools which took part in the survey. Data obtained from heads of mathematics reflected a similar level of use throughout mathematics departments in Northern Ireland.

However, within mathematics departments, the use of computers to help teach mathematics was not widespread. Even in those departments which used computers, less than a quarter of teachers were reported as using computers more than rarely. If those departments which did not use computers at all in their teaching are taken into account, fewer than 10% of all mathematics teachers used computers even on an occasional basis.

Evidence obtained from a small sample of teachers during interviews indicated that those teachers who used microcomputers in their teaching had shorter lengths of service than teachers who did not use them. There was also a strong relationship between teaching computer studies or computer awareness and using computers in mathematics teaching. The majority of teachers who used computers in their teaching had received some inservice training, although only a small number had taken part on courses which focused on the use of microcomputers in mathematics. It is interesting to note that among those teachers who were interviewed there was no difference in computer use between male and female teachers. Similar proportions of both sexes used microcomputers in their mathematics teaching.

These patterns of use might be explained in several ways. Younger teachers may have received some pre-service encouragement to use computers during teacher training or more senior colleagues may have developed a style of teaching over a period of years which they may not be easily persuaded to modify in order to incorporate the computer.

Teachers who also taught computer studies or computer awareness courses will have acquired a degree of familiarity and expertise with computers which will almost certainly have given them the confidence to use computers in their mathematics teaching. These teachers are also perhaps in a better position than other teachers to assess the potential of the microcomputer as a teaching aid.

Although the observed relationship between attendance at computer training courses and computer use in the mathematics classroom may indicate the positive benefits of training, the relationship could also be explained by the speculation that if a teacher had taken part on a course then he or she was probably already interested in using computers. Here, it is interesting to note that the area covered by the Western Education and Library Board, which had the highest proportion of teachers who had been on courses dealing specifically with the use of microcomputers in mathematics, also had the largest proportion of mathematics departments which used microcomputers.

It was found that computer use tended to take place most often with younger pupils and non-examination classes. This was apparent in grammar and secondary schools alike. Reasons for this mainly centred around the pressure of completing examination syllabuses at CSE, O-Level and A-Level, and the availability of appropriate software. These factors are discussed more fully in the next section.

5.4 Factors which inhibited widespread computer use in mathematics

The factors which discouraged computer use among mathematics teachers were found to be predominantly practical. While only 7% of respondents stated that teachers needed to be convinced of the usefulness of computers in the classroom, the majority of departmental heads placed such practicalities as the provision of adequate hardware for class use, the limited availability of good software and lack of training on the applications of microcomputers in the mathematics classroom at the top of their list of discouragements.

Although resource levels had steadily increased since 1980, the problem of computer availability was frequently stated. While many mathematics teachers have usefully and successfully introduced a single machine into their classrooms, the various problems posed by small screens for whole class demonstrations and the further difficulties which arose if pupils were to use the computers themselves or in groups were factors which prohibited use by many mathematics teachers.

An additional problem, posed by having low hardware resources with software designed for individual pupil use, as described by Hennessy (1982), was often emphasised by teachers in Northern Ireland schools.

> "The reality of the classroom situation in which 30 pupils have to share one microcomputer is light years away from the one-child-per-keyboard situation for which most computer based teaching materials have been designed."

Even in schools with larger numbers of computers based in dedicated computer rooms, most teachers reported that there were usually between three and five pupils per computer. While they felt that discussion and interaction between pupils about the mathematical ideas involved in some of the programs were valuable, teachers suggested that, ideally, no more than two pupils should have to share each machine.

In addition to the problem of adequate numbers of computers for class use, departmental heads described difficulties in reserving the room when they needed it because of its use for other subjects, particularly computer studies. This was clearly a management problem and it was apparent that strategies or policies should be developed within schools so that access can be as straightforward as possible for any subject teachers wanting to use this central resource.

Many heads suggested that, if more and better software was available, then more teachers would use computers. It was suggested that most of the currently available software did not fit in with courses being taught and that this discouraged teachers from using the resource. Teachers reported, during interviews and in questionnaires, that they did not have time to invest in the use of computers with examination classes as they had a certain number of essential topics to cover in a finite time. They felt that they could not spare valuable course time to introduce computer based materials which usually did not relate directly to the syllabus being covered. This problem was recognised in a document produced by the Association of Teachers of Mathematics (ATM, 1982) which stated that:

> "Microcomputers will only be used in the classroom if teachers can see the direct relevance of the software to the syllabus that they are teaching."

It was found that teachers felt that current software was lacking in several respects, for instance in its relevance to the syllabus, its educational value, and its reliability. Just under half of the software items listed by departmental heads in this survey were rated as being 'of limited use'. Many pointed out that although there was a supply of programs for younger pupils, there was a lack of suitable software for older and more advanced pupils, in particular those taking A-Level mathematics. Revision software was typically all that was available for pupils beyond the third form stage.

Software has been widely criticised for its quality, as in a recent paper by a sub-committee of the Mathematical Assocation (Hughes *et al.,* 1984), which examined some software in current use in primary schools and with younger pupils in secondary schools. The committee considered the mathematical accuracy of the programs and classified them into three categories:

(a) mathematically sound programs without major problems,

(b) programs which need particular care in use in order to achieve the objectives and to avoid introducing incorrect mathematical ideas, and

(c) programs that have serious mathematical deficiencies.

As an example of one program which the committee felt had serious mathematical deficiencies, this is what it said about VENNMAN, which several departments in this survey mentioned using:

> "The program makes a fundamental mistake in confusing a 'set' with a 'member of a set' and could quickly lead to incorrect mathematical ideas being formed."

Teachers also reported that they, at times, had practical problems with software. For example, some programs proved difficult to get to work, while others sometimes stopped for no apparent reason. Although most teachers said that software quality had improved recently, particularly disk based software, it needed to be thoroughly checked before use in the classroom.

Many heads of mathematics stated that if the available software was more user friendly, that is, if it were easy to use and had simple, straightforward documentation, then teachers would feel more positive about using computers. Others suggested that associated course materials would be useful for incorporating the computer into a scheme of work. This point was also stated in a recent article by Kontos (1984),

> "A CAL package of material must consist of at least a teachers' guide, student notes, and a computer program. The provision of a teachers' guide is of paramount importance. It is the first thing that a teacher will look at before adopting the package."

It was found that many teachers did not know what software was available. During visits to schools, the researcher met teachers who said that they would use computers to cover certain topics if they had appropriate software. The researcher then found, in other schools, teachers using software for those topics.

Although the Education and Library Boards provided catalogues of available software which could be borrowed from them, some teachers were not aware of this. Others felt that the catalogues should appear at regular intervals with some details about the packages. It is clear that, within schools, there should be channels to enable such information to flow to each department. Although this happened in a number of the schools visited, it was suggested that too often such arrangements rely on the goodwill of interested teachers and that more formal dissemination structures should be developed in schools.

The further problem of finding funds to purchase software was evident. Although many teachers borrowed programs from the software library operated by the local Education and Library Board or the MEP regional information centre, they would prefer to establish libraries of good software within their own departments.

The need for appropriate training was widely recognised by participants in the study. Many heads felt that teachers' lack of knowledge about computers and their potential use in mathematics was a strong discouraging factor. Some heads suggested that many teachers lacked confidence and were afraid of using computers. Although approximately one third of mathematics teachers have been on some sort of computer training courses, less than 5% of mathematics teachers had received instruction in the use of computers in mathematics.

The majority of courses attended dealt with aspects of computer studies or computer programming, skills which are not essential to the implementation of computer assisted learning techniques in the classroom. Departmental heads indicated the sorts of courses they felt would be most useful for mathematics teachers. These included more practical courses which would be followed-up at regular intervals, possibly incorporating software exhibitions or workshops in which teachers could try out software. In detailed discussions with teachers, it was found that courses on how to manage the computer in the classroom and organise pupils in the computer room were also sought. Some teachers, particularly in rural areas, felt that local or school based courses should be offered.

Training courses are essential for the successful incorporation and utilisation of computers in the classroom and this was recognised in the Cockcroft Report (1982),

> "The fact that a school possesses one, or several, microcomputers will not of itself improve the teaching of

mathematics . . . if it is to be properly exploited, (we) require teachers who have the necessary knowledge and skill and who have been supplied with, or have had the time to prepare, suitable teaching programs."

If teachers are not trained in the use of microcomputers within their own subject, then the huge potential of the computer as a teaching aid will be lost. The need for appropriate training has been widely recognised, as have the likely consequences of ,a failure to provide such support to teachers. Fears such as these, described by Burghes (1982), were widely found among teachers in 1985,

"I am not so optimistic that the teaching profession will in fact fully utilise this exciting resource. While we clearly have a large number of experts now, are we really successfully educating the whole profession? I have serious doubts, and if we fail to do so successfully, I can image a situation when we have a little used educational resource—micros gathering dust in cupboards!"

5.5 Encouragement to use computers in mathematics

Despite the many practical problems facing mathematics teachers, useful and enthusiastic use of microcomputers was taking place in at least some mathematics departments throughout the province. When asked what factors encouraged teachers to use microcomputers in mathematics, heads did not simply provide the inverse of the discouraging factors. As one might expect, heads suggested that more computers would help, as would better software and more training. However, one of the most common reasons given was the increased motivation and interest of pupils when using computers in their mathematics lessons. This agrees with the finding of Fletcher (1983), who, during visits to mathematics classrooms, noted that the greatest change brought about by the use of computers in mathematics was in the response of pupils,

"Pupils in surprisingly large numbers are finding a joy and zest in some aspects of mathematics which they did not find before."

The computer allowed teachers to cover basic mathematical skills in an enjoyable and often exciting way with many pupils. Software such as Logo allowed pupils to actively explore mathematical relationships. One teacher said that during a lesson with DART, she learned a lot by observing the many different solutions suggested by pupils when trying to write short programs to draw a series of circles.

In addition to this increased interest and motivation of pupils, heads also mentioned the unique capabilities of the microcomputer as reasons why teachers use computers. The graphical facilities and the speed of calculations were uppermost in the responses obtained. Indeed, these factors were reflected in the sorts of topics which teachers said they covered using computers. Commonly mentioned topics included graph work, angles, statistics and probability, co-ordinates and geometry.

Knowing how to use computers in the classroom was mentioned by over one quarter of respondents. Teachers felt that it would be useful if they knew how other teachers in similar settings used computers. Some expressed the view that contact with mathematics teachers using computers would be a source of encouragement. Details of how a computer could be incorporated into particular types of lessons, despite limited resources, were requested by many teachers.

Most teachers interviewed said that they were encouraged to use computers by their head of department, and in a number of cases by another member of the department who was interested in using computers. Forms of encouragement ranged from letting staff know what hardware and software were available in the department to the provision of demonstrations and in-school training sessions, although this only occurred in a few schools. Just under a quarter of departmental heads stated that their department had policies on the use of computers in mathematics. Policy objectives were mainly to help teach mathematics and encourage staff to use computers, although some heads aimed to acquire a range of mathematics software for use by teachers in the classroom and by pupils during individual study.

5.6 Conclusions

In 1984, microcomputers were being used in a broad range of subjects in post-primary schools. However, most use was accounted for by a relatively small number of school subjects. Apart from the use of microcomputers to teach aspects of the new technology through computer studies and computer awareness courses, they were also being used to enhance the learning of traditional subjects in the curriculum. The subject which made most use of computers as a teaching aid, as reported by school principals, was mathematics. Indeed, almost half of the schools which took part reported some use of microcomputers in mathematics teaching.

Many of the unique features of microcomputers, for example their graphics, speed and accuracy of calculation, and their motivating effect on pupils, made them appear useful to many mathematics teachers. However, there were also reports of limiting factors. The main restrictions on the use of computers were shortages of hardware, suitable software and 'human skills'.

It would appear from the information supplied by heads of departments and individual mathematics teachers that the major discouraging factors in the widespread use of computers in mathematics were of a practical nature. In an article, "Is there life after MEP?", Esterson (1984) outlined some of these,

> "The major problems inhibiting the use of microtechnology
> in the classroom are lack of software and, as this problem
> begins to be resolved, the training of teachers in its use and
> in its application to the curriculum."

The information obtained in this survey substantiates Esterson's analysis of the problems involved in educational computing. However, the survey has also drawn attention to more fundamental barriers to the widespread use of computers in schools.

Although many schools now have numbers of computers, some still only have access to one computer, or a few located in different classrooms in the school. While it is possible to have useful lessons using a single computer in a classroom, this restricts children's learning to topics which can be presented by the teacher to the entire class simultaneously. Even then, problems are caused by small display screens and a lack of software designed for this type of use. Teachers also felt that moving computers to their classroom proved inconvenient and often resulted in lost class time. In schools with low resources, teachers were agreed on one major issue. If greater numbers of microcomputers were available, more mathematics teachers would be inclined to use them.

Problems of a different nature occurred in schools which were relatively well resourced. Although teachers valued the facilities provided by dedicated computer rooms, such as having a number of computers available and thus allowing the class to have some degree of 'hands on' experience of using computers, difficulties often arose. Access to the computers was complicated when a number of departments wished to use them at the same time. When a school has acquired a number of computers and these are centrally located in a computer room, careful co-ordination is needed if different classes and subject areas are to benefit, if staff development sessions are to be fitted in and if teachers are to have the opportunity to try out software. While the logistics of such co-ordination are not easy, it is nevertheless essential if the maximum use of the resource is to be achieved.

One teacher suggested the appointment of a specialist within each school as a solution to the management of both hardware and software. This person could be responsible for the resolution of difficulties, both of hardware and software, and could advise staff on available packages and assist with in-school training for staff. It was stressed that such a person, particularly in the computer room, might encourage more teachers to use the resources.

Problems with mathematics software largely related to its quality and suitability for use across a wide range of pupil abilities. Many respondents stated that mathematics teachers did not know about available software and that this hindered further computer use. It was felt that Education and Library Boards which have software libraries should send details of the available software regularly to schools. In a number of schools one or more members of staff acted as a computer adviser and often he or she was responsible for passing such information on to other teachers. There should be similar channels in all schools so that members of staff could be kept informed of new developments.

It was emphasised by teachers that software packages should be user friendly and have simple, though effective, documentation. Teachers agreed that machines fitted with disk drives had resolved many problems with the use of software although there were still some items which proved unreliable and difficult to use with confidence. In schools which had network systems, teachers reported that it was much easier to use the machines with large classes. However, it was also pointed out that several software packages did not work on network systems.

The provision of software for use throughout the age and ability ranges of pupils studying mathematics was considered essential for the continued growth of computer assisted learning in this subject. This study pointed out that the majority of computer use took place with non-examination pupils. Indeed, it has shown that most of the computer use in mathematics involved younger and less able pupils. Similar trends were found in the mathematics departments of both grammar and secondary schools. Despite the different ability ranges within each kind of school, it appeared that in both instances the bottom end of the school had most opportunity to learn mathematics with computers, and that computer assisted learning was largely avoided with classes preparing for public examinations. During interviews, some teachers explained that computers and the current crop of associated materials were only suitable for "playing around" and until better software appeared they would not use the computer for any serious applications.

This situation could be improved by software producers paying closer attention to examination syllabuses and endeavouring to develop programs which would match what was being taught. Further problems with regard to using software, when available, with examination classes included the lack of 'spare' time in busy courses to allow computer use.

Departmental heads and individual teachers identified the need for training in the use of computers among mathematics teachers. Most of the training already received by mathematics teachers had not specifically dealt with the use of computers to enhance the teaching of mathematics. Teachers stressed their need for courses on such practical matters as how to use a single computer with a class, or how to utilise a computer room. Regular courses, exhibitions of available software, and the facility to try out software were often mentioned. There was also a desire for local and preferably school-based training. The teachers felt that specific training of this nature should be of a practical bent so that its benefits could be immediately put to use in the classroom. In a few of the schools visited, members of the mathematics departments were themselves taking action on a 'self help' basis. These teachers were planning to organise some in-school training to encourage those teachers not already using computers and to increase the expertise and awareness among teachers who used computers.

The benefits of training and experience were clearly observed in the study. It was found that most teachers who used computers either had taken part in training courses or had taught courses in either computer studies or computer awareness. There was an indication that the benefits of these kinds of experience were indirect. Familiarity with the technology achieved through training and practice resulted in the perception of the computer as a tool and not as an object to be feared. Many departmental heads suggested that teachers were afraid to use computers, and there was considerable scope to tackle this problem.

Although there are still many problems to be resolved before computer use in mathematics and indeed other subjects is widespread, several instances of good practice were found in this study. Many teachers managed successfully with a single computer in their classroom, while others made effective use of their schools' computer rooms. Within those departments which used computers effectively, there was an obvious enthusiasm among most staff for the benefits of microcomputers. Even in seemingly less-favourable situations, still there was hope for improvement. Almost all teachers interviewed who did not use computers were willing to try them out in a teaching situation. This goodwill could be harnessed if the practical problems already noted were to be tackled in a purposeful approach to making the best use of hardware and introducing software which teachers can use with confidence.

Mathematics teachers were not averse to using computers. Their usefulness was widely recognised, particularly in the motivating effect on pupils. It is therefore essential that appropriate steps are taken promptly to build on the current enthusiasm of teachers, otherwise a most powerful aid to mathematics education may not achieve its full potential. While the potential of the microcomputer as a powerful teaching aid in mathematics remains largely unfulfilled, the findings of this survey have helped to clarify the obstacles and have given some indication of how they might be tackled.

The Main Findings

Chapter One: Introducing the Study

1. Since 1980, with the help of several schemes and funding from a variety of sources, schools have acquired their own computing power.

2. The need for research into the uptake and use of microcomputers in schools has been widely recognised.

3. The Secondary Mathematics Panel of the Queen's University Teachers' Centre asked The Northern Ireland Council for Educational Research (NICER) to investigate the use of microcomputers in post-primary mathematics teaching.

4. A questionnaire was sent to the principal of each post-primary school asking about the availability and use of computers within the school. Replies were obtained from 88% of principals.

5. Heads of mathematics in each school were sent a more detailed questionnaire which sought information on computer use in the department, factors which encouraged and discouraged computer use, and training which staff had received with computers. Over 60% of departmental heads returned questionnaires.

6. Mathematics teachers from a small sample of schools were interviewed about computer use in mathematics teaching.

Chapter Two: The availability and use of microcomputers in Northern Ireland

1. In 1984 the number of microcomputers in each post-primary school in Northern Ireland ranged from one to twenty two. The average number was found to be just over six.

2. Computer availability varied between grammar and secondary schools, across geographical areas and according to school size.

3. The BBC Model B microcomputer was found to be the most common microcomputer in Northern Ireland's post-primary schools. It accounted for almost 60% of all the machines reported and was found in over 90% of schools.

4. The most common location for computers in schools was the computer room. Over 70% of the microcomputers described were held in computer rooms.

5. Just over 40% of principals stated that their schools had a policy on the use of computer assisted learning across the curriculum. In addition to encouraging computer use, the most frequent objectives were to obtain hardware and software, train teachers and introduce pupils to new technology.

6. Although microcomputers were used to teach a wide range of subjects, most use was accounted for by a relatively small group of subjects.

7. Microcomputers were used to teach computer studies and computer awareness. In those schools which did not have computer studies departments, tuition was provided by other departments. In just under one-fifth of schools the mathematics department taught these topics.

Chapter Three: Microcomputer use in mathematics departments

1. Less than half of the mathematics departments which participated reported using computers to help teach mathematics. Within those departments which used microcomputers one quarter of the teachers used computers at least occasionally in their teaching.

2. Microcomputers were used to help teach a wide range of topics. The use of computers with graphical topics was particularly common.

3. Younger pupils and those not taking examinations were more likely to use computers during their mathematics classes.

4. One quarter of departmental heads described policies on the use of computers in the teaching of mathematics in their department. In addition to the general aim of helping to teach mathematics, the most common objective was to encourage staff to use computers in their teaching.

5. Departmental heads stated that such factors as the availability of good software, pupil motivation, the unique characteristics of the computer and the greater availability of computers encouraged mathematics teachers to use computers.

6. Such factors as a lack of computers with large classes, lack of teachers' expertise with computers, lack of software and organisational problems were described as being major discouragements to teachers wishing to use microcomputers in mathematics.

7. Few teachers (one in twenty) had received inservice training on how to use computers to help teach mathematics. Departmental heads suggested that courses should deal specifically with mathematics, be practically oriented and allow teachers to try out software.

8. Departmental heads described and offered suggestions for improvements in the support services provided by Education and Library Boards. In particular they suggested that better contacts should exist between schools and Boards with regard to such services.

Chapter Four: Classroom practice

1. Some teachers successfully used a single computer in the classroom as an "electronic blackboard". However, problems such as the legibility of small computer display screens were often mentioned.

2. When a single computer was available in the classroom, pupils were often allowed to use it in pairs or individually.

3. Teachers mentioned that, if the computer had to be brought from another location to their classroom, class time was often lost while the machine was made ready for use.

4. In computer rooms where larger numbers of machines were generally available classes were divided across all the available machines.

5. Differences in computer use were noted across schools with different resource levels and among individual teachers.

Chapter Five: Summary and discussion

1. The findings highlighted practical problems in the uptake of computers in the teaching of mathematics.

2. Although the need for the development of teacher expertise with computers was recognised, hardware and software deficiencies were obstacles for many teachers.

3. Teachers who did not use computers stated that they would consider using them if the practical problems were resolved.

4. This goodwill and enthusiasm should be harnessed so that the potential offered by this technology is realised.

References

ASSOCIATION OF TEACHERS OF MATHEMATICS (1982). *Working notes on microcomputers in mathematical education.* Derby: ATM.

BBC EDUCATIONAL RESEARCH UNIT (in press). *Microcomputers in Secondary Schools: a survey of England, Wales and Northern Ireland.* London: BBC Data.

BRISSENDEN, T. and DAVIES, A. (1975). Computer Graphics in the Teaching of Science and Mathematics. *Mathematics Teaching,* No. 72, pp 49-54.

BURGHES, D. (1982). Inservice micro courses for the teaching profession. In Smith C. (Ed.) *Microcomputers in Education.* Chichester: Ellis Horwood.

BURNS, P. K. and BOZEMAN, W. C. (1981). Computer Assisted Instruction and mathematics achievement: Is there a relationship? *Educational Technology,* 21, pp 32-39.

COCKCROFT, W. H. (1982). *Mathematics Counts: Report of the Committee of Inquiry into the teaching of mathematics in schools.* London: HMSO.

COUNCIL FOR EDUCATIONAL TECHNOLOGY (1978). *Microelectronics: the implications for education and training.* London: CET.

DEPARTMENT OF EDUCATION AND SCIENCE (1985). *Mathematics from 5 to 16.* Curriculum Matters 3. London: HMSO.

ESTERSON, D. (1984). Is there life after MEP? *Computer Education,* 47, pp 20-22.

FLETCHER, T. J. (1983). *Microcomputers and Mathematics in Schools.* London: Department of Education and Science.

HATIVA, N. (1984). Computer-Guided-Teaching: An effective aid for group instruction. *Computers and Education,* vol. 8, no. 3, pp 293-303.

HENNESSY, K. (1982). A systems approach to curriculum development, the Manchester project for computer studies in schools. In Smith, C. (Ed.) *Microcomputers in Education.* Chichester: Ellis Horwood.

HUGHES, B., DANN, P., FLETCHER, T., INSTONE, S., PERKINS, P. and SWEETON, C. (1984). Microcomputer Software. *Mathematics in Schools.* September, pp 9-10.

KULIK, J. A., BANGERT, R. L. and WILLIAMS, G. W. (1983). Effects of computer based teaching on secondary school students. *Journal of Experimental Psychology,* 75, pp 19-26.

KULIK, J. A., KULIK, C. L. C. and COHEN, P. A. (1980). Effectiveness of computer based college teaching: a meta analysis of findings. *Review of Educational Research,* 50, pp 525–544.

PAPERT, S. (1980). *Mindstorms: Children, Computers and Powerful Ideas.* Sussex: Harvester.

PHILIPS, R. (1982). Teaching Computer-Aided Mathematics. *Educational Computing,* May, pp 28–29.

RIDGWAY, J., BENZIE, D., BURKHARDT, H., COUPLAND, J., FIELD, G., FRASER, R. and PHILIPS, R. (1984). Investigating CAL? *Computers and Education,* vol. 8, no. 1, pp 85–92.

SAGE, M. and SMITH, D. (1983). *Microcomputers in Education: Framework for Research.* London: Social Science Research Council.

WATT, D. (1983). Is Computer Education out of control? *Popular Computing,* vol. 2, no. 10, pp 13–84.

WELSH OFFICE (1984). *Computers in Learning—A survey of current provision and practice in a selection of Welsh secondary schools.* Cardiff: Welsh Office.

APPENDIX 1

A list of microcomputers found in post-primary schools in Northern Ireland

Microcomputer	Number reported	% of all micros (N = 1431)	Number of schools with 1 or more	% of all schools (N = 231)
BBC B	860	60.1	214	92.6
380Z	214	14.9	193	83.5
Apple II	129	9.0	59	25.5
480Z	56	3.9	12	5.2
Spectrum	50	3.5	27	11.7
ZX81	32	2.2	22	9.5
BBC A	23	1.6	16	6.9
Sharp	14	1.0	8	3.4
Apple IIe	10	0.7	5	2.2
CBM Pet	9	0.6	6	2.6
Tandy	7	0.5	5	2.2
ZX80	5	0.3	3	1.3
Vector	5	0.3	1	0.4
Atom	4	0.3	3	1.3
Commodore 64	4	0.3	4	1.7
Electron	3	0.2	3	1.3
CBM 4032	2	0.1	2	0.9
Oric	1	<0.1	1	0.4
Nascom	1	<0.1	1	0.4
Colorgenie	1	<0.1	1	0.4
ITT 2020	1	<0.1	1	0.4

Printed by Nelson & Knox (NI) Ltd
Alexander Road, Belfast

0353.
3/6/86.
N.I.C.E.R.